THE WARRIORS

Religion, Theology, and the Holocaust
Steven T. Katz, *Series Editor*

HAROLD ZISSMAN

THE WARRIORS

MY LIFE AS A JEWISH SOVIET PARTISAN

SYRACUSE UNIVERSITY PRESS

Library of Congress Cataloging-in-Publication Data

Zissman, Harold.
The warriors : my life as a Jewish Soviet partisan / Harold Zissman.— 1st ed.
p. cm.—(Religion, theology, and the Holocaust)
ISBN 0–8156–0839-X (alk. paper)
1. Zissman, Harold. 2. Jews—Poland—Ostrâw Mazowiecka—Biography. 3. World War,
1939–1945—Jewish resistance—Poland. 4. World War, 1939–1945—Jewish resistance—Belarus—
Dzëirçchyn. 5. World War, 1939–1945—Jewish resistance—Soviet Union. 6. Holocaust, Jewish
(1939–1945)—Poland—Personal narratives. 7. Poland—Ethnic relations. 8. Belarus—Ethnic
relations. 9. Soviet Union—Ethnic relations. I. Title. II. Series.
DS135.P63Z599 2005
940.53'47'092—dc22   2005022255

Contents

Illustrations

Preface

FOR THE SAKE OF THOSE READERS who fought in the war alongside me, who are the real witnesses to this story, I must explain my name. I was born in Ostrow-Mazowiecka, Poland, with the name of Hersh (Grysha) Cukierman. At war's end I was drafted into the NKVD (later renamed the KGB). Not long after that, the Soviet government announced through street posters that all those who had lived in Poland before 1939 could now return there, but must first register with the authorities for travel permits.

The offer appealed to me—I was no communist. So without giving it much thought, I followed my poor judgment and registered to return. What a folly that was! My former comrades shunned me like a stranger. My officers all told me to repent, do *something*. "Come back to our side," they all told me. "No harm will come to you."

So I retracted my registration and waited to see what would happen next. By now I sensed that I was being watched. "Escape," I began telling myself, "grab your freedom before you're arrested."

But escape how? I quickly got in touch with my wife, who was working in another town, to tell her about my dilemma. I asked her to tell her father about my situation and explain to him that escape was the only choice. Her brother Eddie must go to the registry office and register as Harold Zissman. In that way I would get a new ID. My father-in-law agreed to this plan; he even had my wife arrange for her own papers under my false name. With these false identities we safely reached Bialystok, Poland, and eventually Lodz, where my new life began. And that is how I went from Cukierman to Zissman.

I have many people to thank for their help and encouragement in bringing this book to life. First of all I wish to apologize to all the people I leave out, those many who at one time or another contributed something and encouraged me to go on writing this book.

My wife, Sonia, gave me the courage to begin. Every night, while the rest of the family was asleep, I would begin to type, on an old manual, for at least three or four hours. My English was not very good, but I was interested mainly in recapturing memories and dates, so I knew enough.

So I had written a book. Now I had to find a publisher, which was even harder, as it turned out. I found a literary agent, but by the time he had finished his work on my manuscript I couldn't even recognize my story. At that point I almost gave up.

Someone recommended an editor to me, and I hired him to work on the manuscript, but again, before he was even half finished I couldn't recognize my own story, so I told him to stop.

Around then we moved to Florida, where I was persuaded to give the book another chance. Our dear and long-time friend Zelda Fuksman got hold of the original manuscript and worked on it for a year. It read much better to me, and again I began looking for a publisher and began hearing the same answers as before. So I looked for another editor, and had it rewritten again, and once more the editor handed back a book I hadn't written.

Then fortune finally smiled. I met a man of great distinction: Professor Alan Berger, Raddock Eminent Scholar Chair of Holocaust Studies and director of Holocaust and Judaic Studies at Florida Atlantic University, who recommended me warmly to Brian McCord, assistant acquisitions editor at Syracuse University Press, who in turn urged me to seek out Matthew Kudelka, a developmental editor who had helped a number of authors in SUP's Holocaust Studies program. I applaud Matthew for doing my memoir justice, for finding in the manuscript the story I tried for so many years to tell.

I also wish to recognize Rabbi Silver of Delray Beach, Florida, who read my original manuscript and rated the story highly, I quote from him: "You wrote an excellent piece of history, worthy to serve as a textbook about the Holocaust; that's the good news. The bad news is, I can't help you publish it." Thank you anyway, Rabbi. Your kind words helped me.

The most important thanks for the last. May the Almighty be blessed for keeping me safe while enduring the ordeal of the Holocaust. I shall remain dedicated and grateful to Him always and forever.

Finally, a plea—Readers, please do not judge too harshly my actions during the war. The enemy was a brutal one and the struggle was for freedom itself. I have left out many stories of cruelty, inhumanity, and atrocity. If my story is different from that of others, it is only because I have tried hard to tell it straight, the way I lived it and the way it happened. So please, leave it to historians to judge me.

Fort Lauderdale, Florida   Harold Cukierman/Zissman,
June 2005   survivor of the Holocaust

Harold Zissman escaped the ghetto and joined the Soviet underground. As a Partisan fighter against the Nazis in World War II, Zissman encountered anti-Semitic enemies among his comrades as well. In 1948, Zissman and his family immigrated to Chicago. After years of sharing his wartime experiences with audiences at schools and organizations, he felt compelled to preserve his story for future generations.

THE WARRIORS

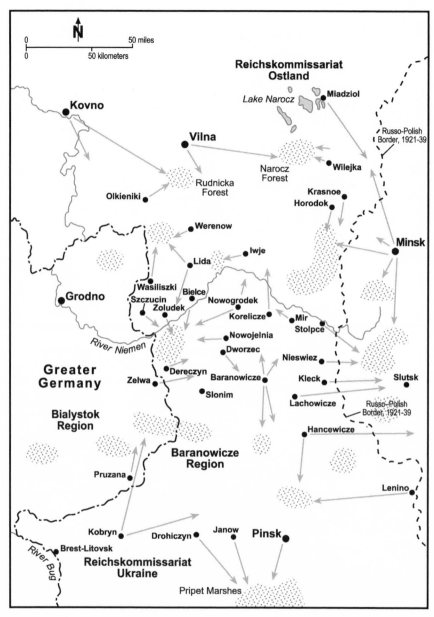

Escape and Resistance, July–December 1943. The movement of Jews escaping towns and villages for forests is indicated by arrows. Adapted from Map 224 © Martin Gilbert. *Routledge Atlas of the Holocaust,* 3rd Edition by Martin Gilbert (ISBN 0415281458 HB and 0415281466 PB, Routledge 2002).

Prologue

SEARCHING MY HEART, I must confess: After I lost my mother as a boy, when I had to look after my brothers and sister while my father was away on business, I didn't show much good judgment.

I was too rough with my brothers, chastising them for not studying or for missing school. Sometimes I would pick fights with them, then later apologize for it. At the time, loving my siblings was more a duty than a kindness.

After losing my entire family in the war and fighting the Nazis for so many years under arms, I felt compelled to restudy the history of the Jews. Hanukkah is the feast to celebrate the survival of hope in adversity, the lighting of candles signaling that victory. The Maccabies, though outnumbered by their enemy, resisted bravely and emerged victorious.

When in despair, don't waver. The pogroms of czarist times were a strong warning that the Jews from that point on must resist their enemies. Alas, most of us decoded this message too late.

When I was incarcerated in a forced labor camp, I saw the first gleam of hope when the Soviet Partisans liberated us. Even that early in the war I wanted to join them, and so did many of my camp mates. Alas, the Partisans rejected our pleas and didn't accept any of us. I didn't stop wanting to join them. Back in the ghetto, a handful of us younger men kept trying to link up with them. We didn't succeed, yet still I hoped.

Still later, while doing conscript labor for the Nazis in the ghetto, I organized twenty-three of my coworkers to escape to the Partisans, wherever we found them. One evening I told my friends to say good-bye to their families, and all hell broke loose among the parents. So we didn't go.

So I decided to escape on my own. And at that point, three of my friends pleaded for the chance join me. In that way my dream became reality, and we were able to escape together and join the Partisans. My heart aches to this day for that group of twenty-three I organized—not one of them survived the liquidation of the Derechin ghetto.

My experience must serve as a memorial to them: When in despair, rise up! Life is worth all the pain, all the sacrifice. Survive! We all must. We're an old nation filled with history. Be brave! Endure!

1

THE TOWN OF MY BIRTH, Ostrow-Mazowiecka, was about sixty kilometers from the German border on the road from Warsaw to Moscow. It was founded in the fifteenth century after Kazimir the Great invited the Jews to come to Poland to help establish commerce and industry.

Most of the Jews of Ostrow-Mazowiecka eked out a living as tradespeople—tailors, cobblers, blacksmiths, teamsters, and jewelers. In the early twentieth century, by which time my family was living there, there were also Jewish businessmen and professionals. Still, we were an oppressed minority in our town: five thousand Jewish souls among the twenty thousand Poles.

Both my parents were born there. My father's father, Yidl Cukierman, begat eight children, my father, Itzche Meier, being the oldest. I remember Grandfather's full, silver-streaked beard—a sage's beard. His wife, my grandmother Asna, died before I was born. In time he remarried, taking a woman named Golde, a quiet woman and a good wife, who, even so, never won our family's love or affection.

My mother, Sureh Roize Seres, was the third of seven children. Of these seven, only two—she and her brother Moishe—never left Poland. Her brother Chaim died before I was born, and the other five crossed the ocean for a better life in the land of promise, America.

The Jews of Ostrow-Mazowiecka lived near their synagogues. There were a number of these and much else besides: a *mikveh* (ritual bath) and a variety of Jewish schools, houses of study, and clubs. The Jewish schools included grade schools and also trilingual modern boys' schools that emphasized Zionism rather than religious observance. There was a *heder*, a school for boys only; the other Hebrew-language school was coeducational. The Shalom Aleichem, a progressive, modern Yiddish school for boys and girls, taught Judaism and Jewish culture. All of these were private schools supported by local Jews. There was also a public school attended mainly by Gentiles.

Ostrow-Mazowiecka's Jews belonged to many contrasting organizations, held a variety of ideological views, and observed their religion with different degrees of strictness. Most young Jews followed their family traditions. Their parents chose their children's schools based on their religious leanings and on what tuition they could afford to pay.

In the town center stood the Ratusz (city hall), which soared above the town's red brick houses. Beside it was a park where, on warm summer evenings, people strolled around an artificial lake. In winter children skated there.

My father, Itzche Meier, was a handsome man of medium height with a muscular build, sparkling black eyes and a jovial disposition. He delighted people with his fine cantor's voice and his gift for telling stories. With his children he was a strict disciplinarian who demanded respect, good behavior, and high accomplishment. A stern look from him, or a few words, were all it took to make us behave. A worldly man, clean-shaven and modern in his dress, he was still his father's son in matters of faith and practice. He was a traveling salesman for a variety of wares—crockery, china, glassware, and the like—and most of his customers were farmers and peasants. All week he traveled from one village to the next, struggling to support his wife and four children. He always returned home for the Sabbath. His absence by no means relaxed our respect for his discipline. Mother had only to say to us, "Wait till your father gets home . . ."

Mother was delicately beautiful. A modern woman and a warm, loving mother, she was dedicated to her four children and to her husband's family. As a token of love and respect, Grandfather Yidl addressed her as his daughter. In the same way, Father's sisters treated her as a sister.

Nuhim Seres, my mother's father, was an Otvotck Hassid who had dedicated his life to the service and love of God and Torah. He was an energetic man, respected by people, with a silvery, waist-long beard. His dark, intelligent eyes had a piercing glint that drew people to him. He was highly educated in Judaism and taught Talmud to the members of his synagogue, who were strictly religious and observed all the commandments. He was fluent and literate not only in Hebrew and Yiddish but also in Polish, German, and Russian.

His wife, my grandmother Ruhtche, died in 1936. I remember her as an aristocratic woman who wore a bejeweled hairpin clip called a *grock*, which earned her the nickname "the Grock." She ran an efficient house and was an elegant lady, yet she didn't consider it beneath her to get down on the floor and give her grandchildren a horsy-ride on her back.

These two unusual people had six children. Four of them—Avreml, Julius, Arthur, and Esther Rivke—ended up in the United States; only Mother and Uncle Moishe remained in Poland. After my grandmother died, Grandfather shared his home with Moishe. He never remarried.

I remember little of my mother's younger sister, Esther, who left for the United States in 1929, when I was seven. After the war she would be the only living witness of my childhood in Ostrow-Mazowiecka.

Mother thrived on her loving relationship with family and community. Her greatest happiness was to be a good wife, mother, and housekeeper. As busy as the housework kept her, she always found time for charitable work, for example, feeding a *boher* (yeshiva student) at our table a number of times a week.

Father and Mother had grown up as neighbors observing the same degree of orthodoxy. To no one's surprise, the match pleased both families. Mother must have wanted the marriage very much, for she gave up the chance to go to America with her younger brother, Aaron. She chaperoned her brother part of the way, and then returned to marry Father.

I was their oldest child, born in 1922. My brother Chaim Motke was born in 1926. Chaim was a cheerful boy, full of energy and curiosity, playful but with little interest in school. My little sister, Asna Gitel, born in 1929, was a beautiful child with long, thick braids and hazel eyes. She tottered around the house doing chores, like a little mother. She was high-spirited and tender-hearted. The youngest of us was Yerachmiel Chaim, born in 1933. He was a sickly boy and clung to Asna for warmth and affection.

When I was three, I started attending *heder*. There were ten other children in the class, and the rabbi taught us religious observance, the prayer book, and the Hebrew language. This part of my education ended after four years, in 1929, when financial difficulties forced us to move to the town of Ostrolenka. Father hoped to establish a new market there for his wares. Mother hoped to give me a good education so that I wouldn't have to travel for a living, like Father did.

My father's father, Yidl, an Amszenov Hassid immersed in the Torah, had lived with us and his other children in Ostrow-Mazowiecka and did not want to be left behind. Besides, he was a partner in my father's business. So he moved with us to Ostrolenka. This move turned out to be hard for all of us. My new school was a real challenge because I had received only a *heder* education in Ostrow. Its curriculum was trilingual, with most subjects taught in Hebrew but arithmetic, history, and geography taught in Polish. Because of my limited prior education, I was assigned to the first grade, but because I excelled in Hebrew and religious studies, Father hired a tutor for the other subjects and I was catapulted into the third grade. By the time I was bar mitzvah, in 1936, I had graduated from grade school. I continued my studies with a private tutor for another two and a half years. Around that time I also joined Hashomer Hadati, the youth wing of Mizrachi, a religious Zionist organization to which my father belonged.

Mizrachi was a Zionist movement, modern and progressive, that worked toward establishing a Jewish state in the land of Israel. Other organizations were more fanatical and more strictly orthodox and believed the Messiah would come to return them to the land of Israel and Jerusalem. In contrast, members of Mizrachi were expected to go and build the land of Israel and cultivate its soil.

Mother was a loving wife and mother who dedicated her whole life to her family. When she died at the age of thirty-nine, all of us were devastated. This loss left me broken, my confidence shattered. While she was alive I felt loved not only by her but also by the entire family. Her kindness, compassion, and charity were widely known, and when she died in the spring of 1937, two rabbis eulogized her—an extraordinary honor to be paid a woman in those days. As young as I was, I realized that she was more than just our mother; her love was felt in the entire community.

Her death left me, a fifteen-year-old boy, suddenly in the role of guardian to my three siblings. I had to grow up very fast and soon had to stop my education to take on household responsibilities. Many times while reciting Kaddish (mourners' prayer) for her, I contemplated my situation and my responsibilities and the fate of my siblings. The most severely affected was little Yerachmiel, who was only four. Grandfather Yidl and plenty of uncles and aunts lived in town, but none of them could replace Mother's loving care.

Grandfather Yidl lived his life and his Judaism as if it were still 1900 and not 1937. He claimed that all the troubles that were befalling the Jews were the result of the new ways of life they were adopting. He was highly critical of his son for embracing modern ways and modern appearances and for encouraging his children in the same direction.

Uncle Avrum Chaim was an accomplished scholar of the scriptures and Talmud, yet he was observant in the same way as my father: he wore modern clothes and had shaved his beard. Grandfather Yidl had no choice but to accept it all, lest he alienate his sons entirely. Uncle Avrum Chaim became my mentor, monitoring my studies and watching me recite the Kaddish. I liked spending time with him discussing our differences. A traditionalist, he believed in the return of the Jews to the promised land for the purpose of rebuilding the holy temple; I was steadfast in my belief that only the pioneering spirit would return the Jews to their homeland. Our differences eventually drew me away from Hashomer Hadati and toward Hashomer Hatzair, with its socialist leanings and call for *aliya*—an "ascent" to the homeland, where a Jewish state would be rebuilt through settlement, cultivation, and land reclamation. My family was distressed by my new attitude and had difficulty accepting it. However, my Zionist aspirations were the least of our worries—the political situation in Poland was deteriorating quickly, Jewish communities were facing enormous pressures, and the economy was in tatters.

In 1935, after the death of the Polish leader Marshall Joseph Pilsudski, the Polish National Party (PPN) began fomenting anti-Semitism among the gentile population. The PPN's approval of boycotts against Jews damaged many businesses, including my father's. To accommodate our gentile customers, we had to change how we did business, for example by staying open during off-hours so that they would not be seen doing business with a Jew.

In 1937, there was a riot in the town of Przytukie. PPN members picketed Jewish establishments, urging passers-by not to buy from Jews. If anyone left a Jewish shop carrying a package, that package was taken from him, sprayed with naphtha, and set on fire. Faced with overt threats to their lives and property, Jews became fearful. Because of these thugs, they were losing their freedom to live and work. Slogans like "Do not buy from a Jew; patronize your own!" and "Jews, go to Palestine!" were open incitements to persecution. Throughout all this, the Polish government looked the other way. The minister of the interior declared that rioting might not be legal, but boycotting was. "It is not the responsibility of the government to police the PPN," he stated.

In response, the Jews intensified their Zionist activities—often clandestinely—establishing yet more organizations for training young people in farming, so that they might go to Palestine to prepare the soil for a true Jewish homeland.

The riots affected our family in Ostrow-Mazowiecka. Grandfather Nuhim asked me to visit that summer. I was glad to go, hoping that spending time with him would help me shake off the depression I still felt over Mother's death.

On a Sunday soon after my arrival, the cadets of the officers' school in Komorov, a suburb of Ostrow-Mazowiecka, began a riot that lasted two whole days. These "brave" young officers were soon joined by the 18th Cavalry Division of the Polish Army; together they attacked Jewish property, singling out bearded Jews for beatings. Grandfather Nuhim, Uncle Moishe, and I hid in a cellar for two days, fearing that my bearded grandfather would become a target of the mob.

We waited anxiously for Passover, but that year the holiday was not what it used to be. Grandfather Yidl wanted us to come to his house for the seder, but Father insisted on holding it in our own house. The housekeeper, with Asna's help, readied everything for our first seder without Mother, but her absence filled us with gloom. We had once celebrated this holiday with light hearts—with songs and recitations of the Hagadah, the story of gaining freedom from slavery in Egypt. Nothing was the same that year—all of us at the table were depressed, morose. I am sure that our tears brought Father to the realization that he needed to establish a secure home for his children.

He decided to hire a permanent housekeeper to care for his family. To me he entrusted the household finances. Although I attended well to that part, the care of the little ones was wanting. Our housekeeper was too old to care for four children and maintain a clean house. After a few months, Father arranged for my cousins Gitel and Mindl to move in and run the house during the week while he was away conducting his business. This seemed to work better, except that Gitel and Mindl, young girls themselves, were much occupied with visiting friends. The evenings were filled with youthful exuberance; songs were sung and laughter echoed in the house. This activity brought a little cheer into my life but was not suitable for my brothers and sisters. I had to tell Father in all honesty that things had been better—for the house and the children—when we had a housekeeper. Father concluded that a more stable and permanent arrangement had to be made.

So one day, right after Passover, Father called me aside and asked me directly how I would feel about his remarrying. Our discussion brought tears to our eyes; both of us were still grieving the loss of my mother. Father reassured me that he loved Mother very much and said that the only way he could honor her memory and perpetuate his love for her was by creating a safe and secure home for her children. If I was willing to accept a stepmother, surely the little ones would follow my example. I told him I was too young to take part in the decision; it would have to be his alone. In truth, I wanted to run and hide from the very thought of his remarrying.

A few weeks later, Father asked me to come to Grandfather Yidl's house to meet a candidate for his wife. I arrived at Grandfather's house at the appointed time, dressed in my good clothes, wanting to make a good impression. After an evening's conversation with the woman, Father asked my opinion. Again we both cried. When we calmed down, we concluded together that she would not be good for our family. For one thing, she had a business in another town, which would mean moving away from our grandparents or depriving the children of a full-time care giver. A few weeks later, Father again summoned me to Grandfather's, where he presented me to a woman named Bella. After we spoke for several hours, she asked whether she could visit our house and meet the younger children. When she came to visit, she immediately showered them with affection. This made me feel less anxious, yet the raw reality that we would be replacing Mother brought fresh tears to my eyes. A few weeks later, Father married Bella in her hometown of Shnadov and brought her home. Bella returned our home to the warm and orderly place it used to be.

Bella was an attractive woman with light brown hair, sparkling eyes, and a gentle demeanor. She was shy and quiet and blushed easily; even so, she knew how to express her feelings through acts of kindness. She showed a genuine affection for me and my brothers and sisters, and she obviously loved and esteemed Father. It was easy to like and respect Bella. Her sincere devotion made the little ones very comfortable, so quite naturally they began to call her Mother. I found it painful to hear, yet she deserved it. Our home started to feel normal again, and

I began hoping to return to my studies and to living like a normal teenager.

2

BUT RETURNING TO NORMAL LIFE was not to be. The Germans were demanding from the Poles a strategic corridor along the Baltic Sea. The Polish government, headed by Shmigly Rydz, replied, "Not even land the size of a button will Poland relinquish to the Germans."

The spring of 1939 arrived, bright and warm. I was looking forward to a carefree summer of fun at the beach. I was seventeen and believed that my life was finally beginning. Now that the home situation had more or less settled down, I hoped I could pay more attention to sports, play, and flirting with girls. It didn't turn out that way. We couldn't relax; too many thugs were on the streets, abusing Jews.

Ostrolenka was 145 kilometers from the German city of Konigsberg. A good road and three railroad lines connected it to Germany through Polish territory, but the Germans wanted a direct link to that city—a land corridor of their own.

In the summer of 1939, Poland began mobilizing. Young people of draft age were called in for training. Poland's Jews were discriminated against in many ways, but not at all when it came to army service. Young Jewish men left for service, leaving anguished parents behind and dreading the anti-Semitism they knew they would encounter in the army. Yet they bit their tongues and committed themselves to fighting the coming evil, hoping they would make a difference.

The Jews greeted the Jewish New Year of 1939 without celebration. We felt nervous and insecure. We listened closely to the radio broadcasts, searching for a glimmer of hope. But it was clear, if we chose to be realistic, that Poland was the next target of the Nazi war machine's expansionist plans.

Ostrolenka had been demolished in the First World War. Many people remembered that and chose to leave it for safer cities. Father had the same worries, so we gathered the barest household necessities and returned to Ostrow-Mazowiecka, where we found a one-room apartment near Grandfather's house. To augment his sales on the road, Father had a wholesale shop in Ostrolenka in partnership with my grandfather Yidl. With war looming, Father worried about what would happen to the merchandise in the Ostrolenka shop while he was in Ostrow-Mazowiecka protecting his family. As soon as Bella and the children were settled in Ostrow-Mazowiecka, Father hired two wagons and returned with me to Ostrolenka to salvage some of his merchandise. He would bring that portion back so that if war started in either place, we would have something to sell to secure our livelihood.

On September 1, 1939, Germany invaded Poland. That was the day we were returning from Ostrolenka. All morning, German planes bombed and strafed Polish targets, civilian and military, without discrimination. Our progress was painfully slow, with so many bridges and highways bombed out. Many times we had to jump from the wagons and run for cover to avoid being strafed. Nightfall brought a reprieve from the planes. With the Polish military having priority of movement, we inched along the side roads, which were congested with civilian traffic. Not until the next day, after thirty-six hours travel (the journey usually took six), did we finally reappear in Ostrow-Mazowiecka.

At daybreak a ripping, thundering noise woke us up—more German air attacks. Jolted from sleep, half-dressed, with bombs whistling overhead, we ran around looking for shelter. There was none to be had.

Around ten in the morning, orders were posted throughout the town that all men between twenty-one and forty-five were to register for military service. This category included Father, who was forty. We were terrified when he left the house to report to the registration center. What would happen to us if they recruited him? We waited anxiously until finally he came back and told us what happened. There had been turmoil and confusion at the registration center. The men who had reported had been put to work digging shelters. Luckily for us, Father had been released and allowed to return home.

On Sunday, September 3, 1939, the third day of the war, rumors began circulating that the railroads and main roads of our city were being bombed. The elders of our family decided to flee Ostrow-Mazowiecka for Stoczek, a small town across the Bug River about thirty kilometers away. Our family had many relatives there, and we hoped it would be safer. Immediately we started preparing for the trip. By evening, the children were packed into the wagons, and we were on our way. The horse trotting lively, we made it halfway before encountering army blockades ordering all traffic to stop. We learned that the bridge over the Bug was to be demolished to slow down the German advance. Everyone was being rerouted; there was no way forward, so we had to return to Ostrow-Mazowiecka.

Back home, we learned that Father's brother-in-law, my uncle Shalom, who had left a few hours earlier, had made it across the bridge to Stoczek, where he met up with his wife, Father's sister Sheyne Rivke. Years later we learned that they weren't so lucky after all—all our relatives in Stoczek were killed when a bomb destroyed their house. We, too, would have been in that house had the bridge been open.

We also learned that city officials were themselves preparing to evacuate and were burning documents in the Ratusz. The city hall, with its lovely park and trees, had been transformed into a maze of trenches and shelters. It looked empty and abandoned, reflecting the tension of war. Its chimney spewing thick black smoke sent chills up my spine. Our army's pronouncements that it would fight to the last man to defend Warsaw sounded empty now. The retreat was on.

Through all this turmoil and uncertainty, the Jews were preparing for the holiest day in their calendar: Rosh Hashanah. Wrapped in their *taleisim* (prayer shawls), men hurried to the synagogues. Their hearts aching, they beseeched the Creator to save them from the approaching horrors. Turmoil erupted in the synagogue when a pack of SS men barged in wielding their rifles. With much yelling, pushing, and shoving, they chased the stunned Jews outside and marched them to the lake across from the Ratusz, where they forced them to dance, and then to wash their automobiles using their prayer shawls for rags. Then they made the men swim in the lake or paddle canoes. Those who did not know how to swim drowned immediately; the ones who did know were forced to swim till exhaustion. Then they, too, drowned.

The Hassidim in our neighborhood decided to hold the holiday prayers in a cellar. They camouflaged the entrance with a dresser, hoping not to be discovered. Their lamentations echoed throughout the building, their tears and supplications more heart-rending than ever. In our house, the day passed without incident. We were simply afraid to set foot outside. But news reached us. We heard that a rabbi who did venture out had been arrested trying to sneak through a synagogue window. He was abused and wounded and eventually shot to death. Jews were being murdered all over town.

With the German occupation came a food shortage, at which point we *had* to leave the house, whatever the risk. With refugees flooding the city, Ostrow-Mazowiecka's population soon tripled. Lines began forming in front of shops; we had to stand in line for hours just to buy a loaf of bread. The merchants weren't sure which currency to accept. How to store the food was another problem; yet another was how to keep it safe from looters during the bombing raids, when everyone had to seek shelter. The farmers were used to bringing their crops into the city for sale; the Germans had barred them from doing this. Any who were brave enough to ignore this edict and who succeeded in entering the city had their goods confiscated if they were caught.

Meanwhile, the Polish police marched up and down the streets, from house to house and shop to shop, demanding that the keys to Jewish establishments be turned over to them. Jews were no longer permitted to own any businesses. One day the German police entered our building; they had come to search for leather goods that supposedly were hidden there. Our apartment was turned upside down. Dishes and furniture were broken, pillows emptied of their feathers, everything torn apart as if a tornado had struck. All of us were ordered to line up outside, men on one side, women and children on the other. On our side we were ordered to count off in fives; if the leather goods weren't found, every sixth one of us would be shot in front of the rest. As the numbers played out, Grandfather Yidl, Father, and I were all to be shot. We were sure this was our end, and we could only pray. It seems that either luck was with us, or God heard our appeals. The leather goods were found in the next building, and we were released.

This first experience of facing death left us in shock, and we began to understand that our lives had no value. The older, more experienced voices tried to reassure us that only front-line soldiers behaved so severely; so it had been in the last war. When Warsaw fell and a civilian government was put in place, life would return to normal. This was a hopeful thought. All of us were looking for some cheering up. Many of us cited the old proverb "To give up hope is to lose the future." Especially for a Hassidic Jew, to lose hope and faith is to betray God's spirit.

Throughout history, the Jews have faced many tyrants and outlived them by remaining faithful to God and cleaving to the power of His miracles. A miracle would surely happen to redeem us now as well—we would outlive this enemy, too. Faith is the belief of Hassidim. The rabbi's ability to reverse evil to good is not questioned. The Hassid does whatever the rabbi tells him. The rabbi is more than a spiritual leader to his followers—he is an intermediary of God's will and his followers' guide. Hassidim are willing to suffer sacrifices, willing to offer their lives for *Kiddush Hashem* (sanctification of God's name). Planted deep in the consciousness of every Hassid is the account in the Bible of Abraham's willingness to sacrifice his son. Death is not to be feared if it serves a religious purpose.

When I was a child, I was surrounded by people of this religious conviction. As a seventeen-year-old I did not dare contradict or argue with my Hassidic grandparents or elders. To minimize religion was unthinkable; even as the bombs were falling I had to join in the daily service, which we held at home instead of in the sanctuary. The sight of Germans cutting the beards of Hassidim with daggers or bayonets wounded my soul. The burning of synagogues and Torahs was obviously the first taste of future acts of terror.

Having survived the first days of the war, my family realized that it had been foolish to relocate to Ostrow-Mazowiecka. Ostrolenka had not suffered nearly as many agonies. Nor was it receiving nearly as many refugees, so it was affected less by food shortages.

The merchandise we had brought to Ostrow-Mazowiecka was stored in a building across the street from a club for high-ranking Polish officials. This club had been transformed into an office of the General Staff. As a result, this building was a prime target and was nearly demolished by the Luftwaffe on the first day of the war.

Our family had been divided while escaping from Ostrolenka for Ostrow-Mazowiecka. Uncle Avrum Chaim's wife, Leah, and their baby had fled to her parents in Sokolov. This was considered a "safe city," being small and of no strategic importance. Now Uncle Avrum Chaim tried to join her there, but he found all the railroads and highways bombed out. So the family started talking about returning to Ostrolenka. Yom Kippur (the Day of Atonement) was approaching, and my deeply religious family wanted to be united for the High Holy Day.

At four in the afternoon on the day we planned to leave, German soldiers—weapons aimed, fingers on triggers, hollering orders—drove all the Jewish men out of their homes. Downstairs we were lined up six abreast and marched to the public high school. The brutes with their rifles and truncheons beat anyone who fell behind. They made us empty our pockets of all personal items. Machine-gun outposts guarded the school building and yard; German soldiers with mounted bayonets were stationed around the complex. The ferocity with which these barbarians treated us—innocent, helpless men—was deeply dispiriting. Suddenly all attention was directed to the balcony, where a tall German officer in a crisp uniform with gleaming buttons shouted at us—first in German, then in Polish—that everyone must observe the curfew from 6 P.M. to 7 A.M. Those who didn't would be shot.

After six in the evening, we were finally released, and we ran home under a hail of machine-gun bullets. My grandfather, my uncles, and I returned home; to our dismay, Father did not. All night we sat up worrying.

Late in the morning Father appeared again and told us what had happened. With the bullets flying, he had thought it safer to hide for the night at a friend's house. Because of the curfew, he could only move during daylight hours, so to get home safely, he had to sit out the night.

Somehow Father was able to bribe a Pole for a travel permit. Even with this permit, the journey to Ostrolenka would be dangerous. The previous day's experience had convinced us that our decision to leave Ostrow-Mazowiecka had been the right one. There was the danger that Poles or Germans would seize our horses and leave us stranded. Even so, we started out the next morning. We stopped to say good-bye to Grandfather Nuhim, Uncle Moishe, Aunt Sima, and their baby, Rachel. It was an emotional parting: they tried to persuade Father to remain, or at least wait for better travel conditions. Unable to change his mind, they made him promise to return as soon as he could.

Father still had some merchandise in Ostrow-Mazowiecka. He gave the storeroom key to Grandfather Nuhim, telling him that if he couldn't return, he was to dispose of the merchandise as he saw fit. Grandfather Nuhim, tears streaming down his face, blessed us and had us kiss the *mezuzah* on his doorpost as we parted. We promised to return and with God's help be reunited.

It was an anxious journey. Our first priority was to keep our horse fed, which was difficult. Feed was expensive and hard to find. We did not have enough hay and had to let the horse pasture instead.

Father made a detour to a small town to check on a cousin who lived there. He was also hoping to learn from the local farmers about conditions in Ostrolenka. The locals told us that the Germans had massacred all the Jews in town on the first day of the occupation. Shocked and in tears, we continued down the road. What did all this mean? Why were we so accursed as to be the target of so much savagery? Father had traveled this road many times and had a number of customers in the villages along it whom he considered friends. So it dismayed him that when he appealed to them for help, for food, they responded with threats. They would report us to the Germans and we'd die like all the rest, they told us.

The road to Ostrolenka was broken by bomb craters, destroyed bridges, and wrecked vehicles and was lined with smoldering buildings. Bodies were strewn around unburied, and the stench of death hung with an oppressive heaviness. The sight of German installations terrified us. We avoided them by keeping to side roads. We didn't want to bring attention to ourselves, to be recognized as Jews. We were able to reach Ostrolenka by curfew. The only damage we saw was a fallen bridge; apparently the retreating Polish army had destroyed it. Like all Jewish homes, ours had been looted. Most of our furniture was gone, but even so, we were glad to be sleeping within our own walls. Yom Kippur was approaching, and our hearts were set on observing this sacred day. Yet none of us thought of fasting—surely the food shortages were stringent enough to please God. More than anything else, we wanted a safe place to pray.

All the synagogues were closed, and the main one had been desecrated. We gathered in the cellar of one of the houses, posting a lookout to warn us of approaching Germans or Polish police. The day passed, and nothing bad happened on our street. We were thankful for this uninterrupted time to meditate and pray. We learned a few days later that the day had been so quiet because the Red Army was only ten kilometers from Ostrolenka.

3

THE GERMAN-SOVIET PACT had divided Poland between these two powers. Ostrolenka was directly on the demarcation line and was being disputed for that reason. The Germans retreated from the town two days after Yom Kippur. At about noon, a Red Army tank followed by a few armored cars dragging light cannon rolled into Ostrolenka. The town's Jews came out en masse to cheer them—we saw them as our liberators. We thought our lives would be safe again. But our joy was short-lived; a few hours later, the Russians left and the Germans came back. The Jews ran for shelter, fearing a massacre as punishment for greeting the Russians so warmly. Rumors of the Red Army's return were flying about, but we were sure that it was only wishful thinking.

Father wanted to inspect the store he had left locked in Ostrow-Mazowiecka. Uncle Avrum Chaim and I went with him. To our great surprise, we found the store in the same condition we had left it in. We entered without intending to open for business, but within half an hour customers began appearing. Father thought it safer not to open shop, and in any case he didn't know what currency to accept, so he tried to close the door. Angered that he wouldn't open, the customers created a commotion, which alerted the Polish police. Father was arrested. No amount of pleading helped, nor did offering to open the business—they took Father away.

Not knowing what else to do, I ran to Grandfather's house. When he heard what had happened, he broke down and wept. Seeing him so distraught, I did the same. Aunt Hanna Lea and her husband, Simha Edel, came running from next door when they heard us. All of us just stood there, frustrated by our powerlessness to save Father. Then and there, Hanna Lea and Simha told us they would be leaving for the Soviet border the next day.

Finally I gathered enough courage to go home and tell my family that Father had been arrested. Bella had only to look at my face to start crying along with me. Then my brothers and sister joined in. We were wailing as if he was already dead, when suddenly he entered the house. Our joy at having him back turned soon enough to tears: he had been beaten black and blue, and he was bloody with lacerations. He told us that after his arrest the police had taken him to the central jail. There the prisoners were forced to clean the jail cells and yard, all the time being beaten, shouted at, and accused of having started the war.

I told Father that Simha had decided to leave the next day for the Russian border. Father thought for a minute and then declared emphatically that there was no point staying longer in Ostrolenka; he said, "We'll leave too." He sent his little brother, Chaim, to tell Grandfather Yidl of this decision and to also tell him to be ready to leave the next day. This was the first time I had ever seen Grandfather not object to a decision made by my father. At that point, I understood the gravity of our situation. Grandfather did not want to lose the chance to escape the Germans. We planned to pack our household goods, hiding some merchandise under our personal possessions.

Very early in the morning, we loaded the wagons and waited for the curfew to lift. Then with Uncle Avrum Chaim and his sister, Aunt Beileh, we went to the shop. While we were taking out our merchandise, looters pushed their way in, grabbing whatever they could and beating us bloody in the process. Two Poles, both of them good customers in better times, joined in, demanding the keys to the shop and threatening to call the Germans. While Father was pleading with them for fairness, I saw Polish police and German soldiers heading in our direction. Thinking fast, I moved the horse and wagon out of sight. Uncle Avrum Chaim and Aunt Beileh remained at the shop, hoping the police would help them save it from the looters, but the Germans demanded to know who the owner was and what these people were doing there. All of Uncle Avrum Chaim's claims were shouted down by the two Poles, who demanded the keys, claiming that they had come to buy merchandise but that the owners wouldn't sell to them. The soldiers and police beat my uncle and aunt and ordered them to get the proprietor. The end result was that the three of us returned home bruised and bloodied.

Fearing for his life, Father did not go to the police. Instead we loaded our remaining possessions onto the wagon and left the house. With curfew approaching, it was too late to leave the same day, so we went to Grandfather's house. From there we would be able to leave town unnoticed.

We did not leave the next day either, because it was Succoth. That day we heard that the Polish army had surrendered and that Warsaw had fallen. Victorious, the Germans marched through the center of town, shattering our hopes. The town's Jews feared more massacres, and tensions were running high. We heard that several Jews had been killed. Others had been chased by the Germans to the city jail; from there they were sent to the destroyed bridge, where they were assigned to clean the streets. Most people hid in cellars and spent the holiday praying. The Germans posted orders giving the Jews ten hours to leave Ostrolenka. Any Jew found in town after the allotted time would be shot. There was no functioning Jewish Council any more. However, a few courageous men acting on behalf of the community risked approaching the German High Command to plead for more time. This plea did not change the German order; everybody had to find a way to leave. There were two options open to us: go to Warsaw or head for the Soviet zone about ten kilometers away. We had heard that the Russian zone was open to us, but we were worried that this rumor might be a Nazi ploy to get us moving.

Life in the city became precarious. There was no time to lose. The choices were few, and decisions had to be made. Succoth being over, and our shop lost, we had no choice but to start out for the border. We knew we had to obey the German order, but with no regular transportation of any sort, we were at a loss regarding how to proceed. At the same time, our family was lucky to still have two wagons and horses.

Quoting the Bible, Grandfather Yidl told us: "It is like in the story told by our patriarch Jacob. When he faced his brother Esau, he divided his camp." So Grandfather divided his family into two groups: his household, Uncle Avrum Chaim and his family, and our immediate family, all piled into one wagon. The second wagon carried the rest of us. While we were fitting everyone into the wagons, we had little time to look back, to dwell on the loss of our settled lives.

The streets were now clogged with wagons. Taking advantage of our flight, the Poles were looting everything they could and threatening to call the Germans if we tried to stop them. We knew we were vulnerable, that if we resisted we might be beaten or killed. The Poles began brawling among themselves like vultures over a carcass. This confirmed to us that we had to leave: we couldn't keep living among these people. We counted ourselves lucky that the looters weren't trying to stop us from leaving. To give us hope, Father said: "Things can only improve from now on. I hope never to return here, where our neighbors have turned openly against us and become our worst enemies, collaborators with the Nazis."

Grandfather's most prized possessions were his Holy Books, scriptures and *mezuzahs,* and these he placed lovingly on the wagon. He wrapped his beard in a shawl so as not to draw attention to himself and place us all in danger. With a prayer for a safe journey on our lips, we left Ostrolenka. We were heading for Lomza, a city thirty-six kilometers away in the Soviet zone.

The roads were badly congested with refugees, who carried their possessions any way they could, on wagons, carriages and pushcarts, even on bicycles. We all rumbled together down the dusty road. The choking haze caked every face with gloom. German patrols were ordering everyone off their wagons and stealing whatever pleased them; Polish civilians were following behind to pick us clean. The roadsides were littered with goods the refugees had discarded along the way. Some of us were severely beaten for trying to hide things from these vultures. They spent little time searching our wagons; we weren't carrying furniture, so it looked like we didn't have much. Thus we were able to continue our escape without further losses or injury. That did not stop us from wishing that Germany's reward would be the fate of the biblical city of Sodom.

We didn't expect the Soviet zone to be any better. But what a refreshing surprise awaited us there! The Soviet border guards were pleasant and welcoming and let us enjoy some hot tea and bread— even cigarettes were available. I looked back on my life: I, Yeshaye Hershel Cukierman, raised from childhood in *heder,* immersed in Jewish tradition, Jewish studies, Jewish lore—what made me abandon all of that and join Hashomer Hatzair? Until now I'd had no time to analyze my feelings. Now, here on Russian soil where we were being welcomed with kindness and offered help, I began to understand what communism promised and what equality meant, and my young mind quickly began absorbing its values. Having crossed the border, we were being treated as human beings, no matter that we were Jews. I began asking myself how this system functioned and what it offered humanity. But there was no time right then for answers. We were across the border. We were safe and being treated with kindness, and that was all that mattered.

Grandfather insisted that we all pray together and thank the Almighty for leading us to safety and allowing us to worship. With his approval, Father decided we would wait where we were for the rest of our family in the second wagon. We were on the main road out of Poland, so surely they would come this way. Our food supplies were running short, so we started looking to replenish them. Having known people in the area before the war, through his business, Father decided to continue on to a nearby village. We came to a house where Father used to conduct business and found everything locked up. This area had also been under the Germans for a while, so we were worried about the fate of these people. We stopped to graze our horses. After a few hours, the second wagon caught up with us. Our joy at being re-united lifted our spirits, and together we thanked the Almighty. We were together again in a familiar town, Shnadov, the hometown of our stepmother. Bella's sister welcomed us warmly, but there was no room for all of us to stay, so we had to split up again.

Many relatives on Grandfather Yidl's side lived nearby in Jed-wabno, so my uncles and aunts took Grandfather there, hoping to find accommodation for our large contingent. It was agreed that after a cou-ple of days' rest, we would all meet in Jedwabno. So our two wagons continued; only our immediate family and cousin Simha, Uncle Hirsh's son, stayed with Bella's sister.

We were astonished that a handful of kilometers made so much dif-ference. The Russians had taken the town back before the Germans could do their evil. Grandfather told us that the Almighty was looking out for us, and he compared our journey to the Exodus. He was espe-cially glad that he could pray again without fear. His enthusiasm and unwavering faith filled me with hope.

Refugees from the German zone, some from Ostrow-Mazowiecka, were pouring into Shnadov. They told us that the borders weren't yet sealed off and that the Germans had installed a Polish puppet govern-ment to administer the town. Hearing this, Father decided that we had to try to retrieve our merchandise from Ostrow-Mazowiecka. From the stories people were telling us, this attempt would certainly be dangerous, but Father was consumed with the need to provide for his family. Bella's brother Duvid thought of a daring plan and volunteered to help carry it out. We would dress like Polish peasants—the Poles weren't restricted in their movements—get two farm wagons, load them with potatoes and wheat, and pretend to be taking these sacks to the mills in Ostrow-Mazowiecka. Father, man of action that he was, hired two wagons to get this daring scheme underway. He and Duvid would drive the first wagon, Simha and I the second. Examining ourselves, we wondered whether our peasant clothes would pass scrutiny. We resolved to be brave, and to speak no Yiddish even on the Russian side.

We started early the next morning. The sun was bright, casting long shadows on the side roads. The warm breeze felt reassuring. To our surprise, there were no German patrols at the demarcation line, and we were able to cross into the German zone undisturbed. At that point we separated, planning to meet at Grandfather's house.

Simha and I traveled along the back roads and through private lanes and arrived at Grandfather Nuhim's house in Ostrow-Mazowiecka. We were the first to arrive there. We were happy to see our relatives, and they us, notwithstanding our worry for Father's safety. But he and Duvid arrived soon enough, and we were able to rejoice together in the success of our journey. Father made Grandfather Nuhim and Uncle Moishe promise they would cross the border as soon as they could and meet us in Jedwabno.

We again traveled through the back streets and private lanes toward the storeroom where we had hidden our merchandise. We left one wagon at a distance. Then Father went to ask his friend Mendel Duvid whether the Germans had discovered the merchandise. Surprised and glad to see us, Mendel Duvid told us the things were still hidden, but that German patrols were heavy, morning and evening. We must not be seen opening the storage room.

Although it was almost curfew, we proceeded toward the storeroom. Simha checked the street but saw no patrol. Right away we began loading the first wagon with the most valuable merchandise. Having done so, we parked the wagon in a field behind the building and let the horses graze while we pulled up the second wagon. Again Simha went to check for patrols, and this time he reported one German soldier across the street, some distance away. Father decided to continue loading the wagon. By the time it was half full, the soldier was approaching to see what we were doing. Did we have a permit? Thinking fast, Father told him we were Poles and were taking the merchandise to our store at the other end of town. The German ordered us to wait while he fetched his superior. As soon as the soldier left, Father told us to drive the half-full wagon directly to the Russian border and not to stop until we were across.

How we summoned the courage to carry out this plan I will never know. But we drove the wagon along the back roads and lanes and crossed into the Soviet zone without incident. There we stopped on the roadside to wait for Father. We didn't have to wait long; soon we spotted his wagon rolling across the border. Our success in carrying out our plan, and our relief at escaping the danger, made us feel invincible. This time it was Father who declared that we must humble ourselves and give thanks to God for sparing us from disaster.

By the time we returned to the village we were giddy with laughter and as proud of ourselves as the bravest warriors. We felt drunk with our own courage, especially after so many harrowing months under the Germans. Our family came running and greeted us proudly. That night at dinner, we toasted our success with vodka. Again it was Father who brought us down to earth by reminding us how many of our relatives and friends were still suffering in the other zone, living in constant danger. We were exhausted, and we bedded down as best we could, but sleep would not come to my tired eyes. The thought of my pious grandfather Nuhim and my gentle uncle Moishe under the heel of the German war machine would not let me sleep. Would we ever see each other again?

4

THE NEXT DAYS DRAGGED, the mood somber. It was hard to accept that just a few kilometers away life had no value, a person had no control over his life, and his fate was completely in the hands of the Germans, while here, just across an invisible line, life could be full and happy. Young people were embracing the Soviets, enjoying their freedom, and celebrating that freedom through music, dance, posters, and banners. Eager to learn the language, the ideology, the equality, and the camaraderie, I let myself be swept along. The Red Army's displays of might were very impressive. They raised morale and encouraged enthusiasm. Directed at the young were slogans promising opportunities to develop one's full capacities. The Red Army liberators were the ambassadors of all this promise. They enticed young people with nightly entertainments and speeches at the Dom Krasneyi Army (DKM, or Red Army House). Having endured two years of oppression under the Polish anti-Semitic government before the war, and the more recent German atrocities, I welcomed all these promises of freedom.

We remained in Shnadov until Grandfather Nahum arrived with our Ostrow-Mazowieck relatives. The ordeals under the Nazis had compelled him to follow us. It was good finally to have the whole family together and not be worrying about everyone's safety. That same day we hired two wagons to take the entire family to Jedwabno, where my father's father, Yidl, and other family members had already settled in small apartments. Within a couple of days, Father had settled us in two rooms and found another two-room apartment for my mother's father, Nahum, and his family. Refugees were still pouring in, and housing was at a premium. Most people chose to stay close to their old hometowns, so that when the war ended they would be able to return quickly. People still believed the war wouldn't last long.

Father wanted very much to bring some order to our lives, so he enrolled all of his children, including me, in the local school. Most of the subjects were taught in Yiddish, but that language was dramatically different in this zone. Different spellings were used, Hebrew words had been eliminated, and nowhere in the curriculum were there any references to Zionism. At seventeen, advanced in my studies, I was placed in the ninth grade of the ten-year program. Every student had to learn the constitution of the USSR. The brightest students were inducted into the Komsomol, the communist youth organization. Extracurricular activities, be they sports or youth organizations, were mandatory. Students with mechanical abilities or who wanted to learn a trade were offered places in vocational or mechanical schools. Most students accepted at these schools were entitled to room and board and a small stipend. They could also choose where in the country or in occupied Europe they would attend. The authorities did not use the term "occupied countries"; instead they referred to "liberated lands."

The political seduction, the pressure to be grateful, the generosity of our reception, and the offer of free education made me feel guilty. I didn't want to participate, and I refused to help the Motherland. But no excuses were accepted for not participating, and it was considered a sign of moral weakness to offer any. To stick to the old oppressive ways was disloyal. The march and tempo of life swept the people along, with no allowances made for personal feelings or choices.

The New Year of 1940 was upon us. It certainly was "new"—a new language, a new system, new thinking, new social standards. All of these things affected me deeply. In this atmosphere I was growing to adulthood. I noticed how much importance people accorded to uniforms and medals, and it threatened my self-esteem that I had none. Also, the girls didn't flirt with boys in civilian clothes. Public feeling had been mobilized to promote the communist system. So the New Year was celebrated by cheering, the firing of guns, and the glorification of Stalin and his Red Army.

The spring of 1940 brought new regulations for refugees. All of us who had settled in "liberated" Poland had to accept Soviet citizenship and move at least one hundred kilometers from the German zone. And we were forbidden to live in any large city. Furthermore, we were to vote on whether we wished to become a Polish Soviet Socialist Republic or join the Belarus Republic. This election was the first one I had ever seen conducted under the Soviets. The result was cooked, and the Russian zone of Poland joined Belarus. It was astonishing to listen to the applause that followed this announcement. It wasn't what the refugees had wanted.

Notices were posted encouraging us to become Soviet citizens. Those who did not want to do this were to register for permits to return to Poland and would be advised when they could leave. Some Jews were willing to suffer under the Germans again in order to be reunited with their families and to be able to practice their religion again. The registration seemed innocent enough; in fact, the Soviet authorities later used the resulting lists to round up people in the middle of the night and ship them to Siberia.

Grandfather Nahum and I did not register. The plan was for the two of us to go to Vilna to apply for American visas and seek passage to the United States. We had heard that the U.S. consulate in Vilna was still open and that it was still possible to emigrate. Grandfather told Father that he was too old to go abroad and was sure I could do it on my own. Father wasn't sure if I was mature enough to travel by myself. The arguments between them forestalled any action.

We did not take out Soviet passports until we were summoned to the Passport Office. Grandfather Nahum acted as our spokesman and tried to explain our delay in registering. We were kept waiting for over an hour and finally were shown into a room where a Soviet Army captain angrily accused us of being enemies of the state, ungrateful for the opportunity of becoming Soviet citizens. Grandfather tried to reason with him, admitting our ignorance; he had thought that accepting citizenship was a matter of choice, not compulsion. The captain gave us two hours to choose between accepting a passport and being arrested. Of course we complied, and left the office with passports in hand.

Now that we had our passports, and now that occupied Poland had been annexed to Belarus, we had to comply with any relocation orders. The Soviets told us where we, as refugees, would be permitted to settle.

We could also register for factory work in specific towns, and we would be provided with transportation.

We didn't know how to choose our next destination. One thing was clear: we didn't want to go deeper into Russia. We were still hoping that the war would end soon and we would be able to return home. Better to stay as close to the border as possible. Meanwhile, Father kept selling the merchandise he had salvaged from Ostrow-Mazowiecka and was able to collect some of the money owed him by customers in the area. This income kept us going for a while, and we were able to pay our rent and buy food.

The end of May 1940 was the deadline for leaving the border towns. Again we were being forced to split up our family. We would also be losing the opportunity to continue trading with Father's old customers. How, then, would he provide for his family? But all refugees had to obey the law, with no exceptions. We had been given three choices for our next move: Slonim, Baranovich, or Novogrodek. So we fanned out to explore these areas and choose the most likely one.

The fall of France in the spring of 1940 convinced us that an early return to our homes was unlikely and that we had better throw in our lot with the Soviets and accept them as our liberators. Refugees required special permits to go in search of suitable places for relocation, and with travel restricted, these permits weren't granted without good reason. The new orders also required that all people be gainfully employed. However, it was each individual's responsibility to find a job.

An unemployed person would be summoned by the NKVD (secret police) for interrogation and made to explain how he survived without a job. It did not take much to be pronounced a capitalist smuggler—an activity punishable by exile to Siberia. Black marketeering was a capital offense. For engaging in it, entire families had been sent to Siberian slave-labor camps in freight cars.

The Soviets had kept the borders open and enabled Jews to escape the Nazi menace, and for this we were grateful, but they were unable to provide the most basic needs. People tried hard to adjust and accept the new ways, but often it just wasn't possible. Many refugees who had relocated and complied with work orders returned telling of horrible working conditions, minimal pay, and decrepit housing. In these circumstances, black marketeering was a dangerous necessity.

Our family chose to resettle in Belarus rather than go deeper into Russia. My two uncles and I set out for the city of Volkovysk, where one of our relatives had settled. Volkovysk was crowded with refugees, making it difficult to find shelter. So we continued on to Slonim. Luckily for us, right after we arrived at the train station, through which hundreds of refugees passed, we met a cousin of my mother. With so much overcrowding, we were glad for a place to sleep that night.

The next day, heeding cousin Chaim's advice, we went looking for a place to stay in Derechin, near Slonim, a village of five thousand souls: Byelorussians, Poles, and Jews. Derechin was off the beaten path. Its streets, mostly unpaved, were lined with single-story wooden houses with thatched roofs. It wasn't accustomed to visitors. Our carriage, which brought us from the nearest railway station (Zelva), drew a crowd of villagers as well as the Soviet militia. After being questioned briefly by the militia, we were directed to the housing officer at the village hall. We learned there that the only way to arrange housing was by finding a family willing to share space with us. The official suggested we go from house to house.

As we did so, the people stared at us, hardly able to understand the Yiddish we spoke. Eventually we came to the village synagogue, which, to our amazement, was still functioning. The local rabbi, Bakalchuk, introduced himself and asked where we were from. It raised our hopes that few refugees had come this way. The people gathered around us, curious to hear about our flight and the German atrocities. The rabbi, a kind and gentle man, listened to our story and immediately offered us one room in his house. The other men listening urged us to return with our families and promised to make room for all of us.

Walking to the rabbi's house, we heard music wafting from the Red Army House, where, according to our hosts, a youth dance was held almost every night. People were out strolling, and the warm spring air was refreshing. There was a lazy calmness here; the dangers of the outside world hadn't reached this place. After all we had seen and felt, we were astonished to find a place so relaxed and quiet.

The rabbi and his family extended us a warm welcome. We were invited to wash up and join them in a plentiful supper. We felt lucky. In the morning, after prayers and breakfast, we left for Jedwabno, anxious to bring our families to Derechin before the deadline and in time for Passover.

When we told our families about our warm reception in Derechin, they were relieved and excited. Grandfather Yidl and Uncle Avrum Chaim, the most religiously observant in our family, were glad to hear that a synagogue was still open there and that we had met its rabbi. Surely the Almighty had pointed us toward this destiny. Everybody was anxious to start packing. Even Grandfather Nahum agreed to join us.

There were seven families in our group. We packed all our bundles, including some furniture, onto our two wagons and started out. Father and Uncle Shalom Hirsh, along with another uncle and cousin, drove the wagons, with Father leading the way because he knew this area well. The rest of us found places on a freight car at the railway station. For us young ones, the train trip was a great adventure. At a stopover in Volkovysk, four of us decided to visit our cousin Yitzhak and his family, who lived there. Happy together, we lost track of the time and missed our train. Without any money we would have to struggle to reach our families in Zelva. When we finally caught up with them the next day in Zelva, the adults didn't punish us as we deserved. They were too glad we were safe.

The next problem was how to get ourselves and our possessions from Zelva to Derechin. It wasn't possible to hire more wagons. We had to camp out for several days and nights while our two wagons traveled back and forth. But we were lucky; the days were mellow and the night breezes warm, so it was no hardship to cook and sleep under the stars. For the young people it was a carefree time; it was the adults who longed for a return to normal life.

In Derechin, Father found an abandoned harness shop and moved his family in. It was a dark room with only two small windows. We set up a wardrobe, two folding cots, and a small table with four chairs, and the six of us settled in. Our landlord let us cook in his kitchen. Grandfather Nahum, with Uncle Moishe and his wife and baby, settled into a larger room in a widow's house. Grandfather Yidl, step-grandmother Golde, Uncle Avrum Chaim, and Aunt Beileh with her husband, Anach, and her baby rented two and a half rooms from a gentile family. Aunt Sheyne Rivke and her husband, Shalom Hirsh, our first cousins, with their four children (one of whom had a wife and baby) found two and a half rooms.

It was two weeks before Passover, and we had no matzos to observe the holiday. Even though circumstances were rough, Father took upon himself the great task of baking matzo. The communist strictures against religion were not yet being enforced in Derechin; even so, Father was taking a chance. All the young cousins were recruited to help him. It was only a two-week undertaking, but we could not wait for the holiday to start and the matzo-baking venture to be over. It turned out to be much harder work than we expected or were used to. Immersed in this work, white with flour from head to toe, my head filled with thoughts of the holiday's significance and of the difficult times in which we lived.

The seder was held in Grandfather Yidl's rooms. Its mood was no different from past years. We sang the beautiful old songs and prayers. The seder followed the prescribed order, just as it had for generations. Uncle Avrum Chaim compared our own miracles to those that God had performed for us in Egypt. He explained the meaning of *Ha Lahma Ania* (the bread of affliction) and other passages. He reminded us to be grateful for the miracles that God had always performed for us throughout the ages. We must appreciate the shelter we had found and the opportunity we now had to celebrate the holiday together. It warmed our hearts that night to bask in the faith and strength of our elders. It felt good to watch them draw strength from preceding generations to reinforce their faith. I hoped that we young people would also find the strength and the opportunity to continue our tradition.

5

TO AVOID BEING CONSIDERED CAPITALISTS, which would have placed us in danger of Siberia, Father reported to the Derechin Labor Office with his horse and wagon, claiming to have been a wagon driver in Poland. This was a wise approach. He was hired to haul logs, and I was registered as his assistant. Dense forests surrounded Derechin, and logging was the main industry. The next day, as we rode our wagon down a forest lane, the scent of pine trees and damp earth filled our noses and brought back memories of happy times on summer outings near Ostrow-Mazowiecka. Father was worried that it would be difficult at the logging camp for us to follow the precepts of our religion, but he did not share these worries with me. The only thing he did warn me about was not to discuss politics or ideology, and not to argue with anyone—I should just do the best I could on the job.

We were lucky again; our foreman at the logging camp was a Jew from Slonim, and he was glad to see fellow Jews. He found our wagon unfit for hauling heavy logs, so he assigned us to carry smaller, precut pieces of timber to the Shchara River. From there they would be floated down to the mills.

After two weeks in the forest, Father fell sick with dysentery and had to return to Derechin. When he recovered, he was fortunate to be reassigned to other work. He encouraged me to remain in the forest, to try to develop some trading with the local farmers. The items in our possession could be bartered for food staples. Barter was flourishing. Exchanging goods for goods was not as serious a crime as black marketeering for money.

Following Father's advice, I remained in the forest. This move proved helpful to the family, for I was able to barter for some food. The job, however, was extremely hard, not only physically but also emotionally. It was difficult being a Jew out there in the forest. The Soviets claimed that all citizens were equal, regardless of their race or religion. They were anything but that. I was young, and I tried hard to fit in, to live the promises of freedom and equality, but the Russian laborers did not stop bullying me, the Jew. They labeled every Jew "Abraham" and mimicked our accent, rolling their r's to annoy us. Whenever we Jews had to fell an especially tall tree, a circle of spectators would stand around and jeer at our efforts.

After a few too many such incidents, I appealed to the foreman. He suggested that I write a complaint to headquarters about this treatment, and he asked me if I wanted to be transferred to another group. No, I told him—I wanted be assigned to work side by side with the jeering gentile crew. I felt I had to prove that a Jew could perform this work as well as any Gentile.

The next morning I was assigned to work with one of my tormentors, who soon started the usual degradations. The man complained to the foreman that he would fail to meet his quota because of me. The foreman told him to hold back his complaint until the end of the day.

That day was a hard one, and my partner predicted that I wouldn't be able to continue the next day. Under normal circumstances, he would have been right; my hands were blistered, the pain was unbearable, and I could not hold an axe. But this had become a personal war. I had to prove myself, and I did. I accomplished what I set out to do: I gained my workmate's respect. From that day on, the working conditions improved.

I spent most of that summer cutting trees around Derechin while Father transported scrap metal from Derechin to Slonim. The trips to Slonim three times a week opened an opportunity for Father to earn some extra money by taking passengers. My bartering around the forest kept us supplied with food, some of which Father exchanged for other goods. Together, then, we were able to support our family.

We had just settled down when I was transferred to the turpentine factory. This was even harder work and completely alien to me. It involved enduring extreme heat and fumes while loading tree roots into furnaces to extract the turpentine, then reloading these roots into another furnace to extract tar, and finally processing the roots into lump charcoal. I was determined to prove myself again. By the end of summer, I was able to secure a transfer to work with Father as his assistant in transporting scrap metal.

While working in the forests and the turpentine factory, I established contacts with many farmers, who came to depend on me for salt, sugar, naphtha, sewing items, and other useful goods. They provided food in exchange. By then the farmers knew where I lived, and they would come to the house with their goods and pick up what they needed. At that point, Father asked me to stop bartering for a while. We would try to manage without taking chances. The risk of being caught was great, and the punishment was immediate deportation to Siberia.

My job as Father's helper was very hard and unpleasant because it involved traveling by night. I became isolated from other young people, with no diversions in my life. The pay did not meet even the most meager needs. After a couple of months, I accepted a job at a construction project in Horoszcz, a town near Bialystok. A huge barracks was being built there. The work was being done by a few thousand unskilled civilians supervised by military men. The laborers were assigned to different jobs every day. The pay was based on the quantity of production—for example, how much cement one could mix or how many bricks one could unload. We had to use machinery that none of us had ever seen, much less operated, so learning slowed production, and pay followed production. Our living conditions were primitive. We were housed in military barracks and slept in bunks. The adjoining dining room sat two hundred people at a time. The washroom was a filthy communal outhouse. The pay was barely enough for other needs—shaving soap, razor blades, beer, and snacks—and these weren't always available. Sometimes we were permitted to visit Bialystok, for which free transportation was provided.

After a couple of months, I arranged a pass to return to Derechin. Father was thrilled to see me, and he prodded me to find another job and not to return to Horoszcz. I was able to get back my job as his assistant. I was also determined to start bartering again, regardless of the consequences. I renewed my contacts and was able to help feed our family again. All of our relatives struggled in the same manner to survive, except for Grandfather Yidl, who was supported by his children, and Grandfather Nahum, who received clothing parcels from his children in America. He traded or sold these clothes to support himself.

The winter of 1940–41 fell harshly on us. The temperature fell lower than most years, and the snow fell more heavily, and the roads were hard to get through. Father kept hauling scrap and, of course, always had passengers who were going to Slonim to trade.

I will always remember February 5, 1941, as a sorrowful day. After a week stranded in Derechin by the weather, Father decided to attempt a trip to Slonim, taking with him his usual passengers, including his good friend Krimolowsky. They left around eight in the evening. By ten, he and his passengers had returned: the roads were too difficult and the horse had refused to go beyond a certain spot. Father judged that the load had been too much for the horse in these harsh conditions; he had taken pity on the animal and come back. His passengers then persuaded him to leave the load behind and take just them. They promised him that if the same difficulty arose, they would get off and walk.

So they started again without the load, and at exactly the same spot the horse again refused to move. The passengers got off the sled, but the horse still refused to continue. Father had never needed to whip the horse; it had always had obeyed his voice and hand signals. That evening he cut a strip of cloth to use as a whip. When he applied it, the horse reared up and kicked Father in the lower abdomen. Father fell to the ground, crying out in pain. Krimolowsky rushed to his side and, with the other passengers, gently placed him on the sled. Then, to everyone's amazement, the horse pulled the sled with all the passengers back home.

After Father left for Slonim the second time, an ominous sensation that I couldn't explain had penetrated my being. I felt agitated and couldn't sleep. Around two in the morning I heard a horse and sled in the street. My heart pounding, I dressed quickly and ran out. Father was in severe pain. Krimolowsky yelled for me to get the doctor while he carried Father into the house. Realizing that Father was badly injured, I hopped onto the sled and sped to Dr. Rosenzweig's house.

Tears streaming down my face, I begged the doctor to hurry. Then I galloped the horse all the way home, wanting to be at Father's side. Dr. Rosenzweig's calming words did very little to ease my distress. He examined Father and ordered us to transport him to the hospital. We had to proceed very carefully and slowly to keep the ride as free of jolts as possible. Father's moans of agony pierced our hearts; we were helpless to ease his suffering. The ride of a few kilometers seemed endless.

By nine in the morning the doctors had decided that Father needed special surgery. The hospital in Derechin was not equipped for it. We needed to transport Father by ambulance to a larger hospital in Slonim. The only ambulance available belonged to the Red Army base. Bella, Uncle Avrum Chaim, and I pleaded with the commander but he refused to help us. We were told it would take days to get an ambulance diverted to Derechin. The hospital would not let any of us stay with Father overnight. When we returned in the morning, we learned that he had died in the night, alone.

The village was overwhelmed by Father's death. To me it was more than a personal tragedy; it also awakened me to the realities of Soviet rule. Under them, equality meant the right to suffer equally.

Bella's sister came while we sat *shive* (the customary seven days of mourning). Now that Bella had lost her husband, her sister told us, she was no longer bound to us—she could return to her family in Shnadov. The children and I were welcome to come along, but that decision was mine. At eighteen, I was suddenly the head of our household. I chose to remain in Derechin near our grandparents and family. At least for now, Bella chose to stay with us.

I came to the sober realization that head of household was more than a title; it made me responsible for providing for our family. My low-paying job certainly wouldn't be enough to meet our basic needs; I would have to keep trading on the black market. The risks would be great, with Siberia a constant threat.

Father's death shattered my spirit. I tried very hard to show my respect and appreciation to Bella and to help her in every way. The little ones missed Father, but they were also deeply attached to their stepmother and loved her as their own. Many times I saw Bella weeping. In a choked voice she would lament, "Why did God take away my good husband, the father of these innocent children?" It broke my heart to listen, and it intensified my own suffering.

The bitter winter continued. The snow and the cold were brutal. Our clothes weren't fit for these conditions, and even if we'd had the money for warmer, there weren't any to buy. All we could do was register at the government store for a clothing allotment and wait. The other option was to buy material on the black market and pay a tailor to sew garments for us.

Then spring came and lifted our spirits. The longer, warmer days and the blooming trees and flowers awakened hopes for better days. Bella suggested that I spend more time with the other village youths, but I refused because the year of mourning for Father hadn't ended. Instead I spent my free time visiting our relatives. Sometimes I was tempted to attend concerts or dance with a girl. I bemoaned my fate: Why was I so unfortunate? Why at my age did I have to struggle so hard to survive? I found no answers. I often remembered Ostrolenka, and my memories of the Nazi occupation brought me back to reality. This was no time to be acting young.

One day in the spring of 1941, a strong wind blew. It was a pleasant, warm spring wind, but it brought tragedy and devastation to our household. A fire had started somewhere down the road, and the wind was fanning it toward our house. The fire consumed the building and all our belongings. Luckily, Bella came back from the market in time to wake me, and we were able to get everyone out. In a daze, I grabbed my pants and jacket. When I returned to my senses I realized I had grabbed the wrong jacket and that all our money was lost. We were just grateful to have escaped with our lives.

The fire had destroyed one-third of Derechin. Scores of people were now desperately searching for housing. Our only option was to separate and move in with our grandparents. Bella suggested that now was the time for her to accept her sister's offer to move to Shnadov. It would be too painful for the rest of us to move away from our grandparents, so we would remain in Derechin. This change was very difficult for all of us, especially for my brothers and sister.

I continued with my trading and was able to provide my siblings with food and necessities. Soon after Bella left, I stopped at my grandparents' to say good-bye before setting out on a bartering expedition. I was always worried I might get arrested and never see them again. Grandfather Yidl was very ill at that time. I offered to stay, but he told me to go, only cautioning me to be careful. Even so, I shortened the trip and rushed back to his side. To my great distress, I found him much worse. My heart breaking, I faced what would be Grandfather's final hours. He saw me enter the room and beckoned me to sit by his side. He reached out and caressed my face with his cool, delicate hands. His eyes smiled at me with pride and love. For the first time in my life, I felt my grandfather's face close to mine. When I leaned down to kiss him, he pressed his face into mine. Quietly, as his life had been quiet, Grandfather Yidl passed away.

Our family suffered yet another tragedy that May. Uncle Moishe's wife, Sima, died, leaving him with a three-year-old girl. These losses added to our oppression, and I didn't know what to say when the children asked me why these things were happening. We could not know that these deaths would soon seem like a blessing. At least Father, Grandfather Yidl, and Sima had proper Jewish funerals and marked graves.

Our mourning for Grandfather Yidl and Sima did not last long. Rumors were circulating that the war was advancing toward us. There was an unexplainable tension in the air.

6

SUNDAY, JUNE 22, 1941, had been declared the day the victims of the Derechin fire would be able to buy replacement clothing and household goods at reasonable prices. As we stood in the store waiting our turn, an announcement came over the loudspeaker that the Germans had attacked the Soviet Union. This announcement was followed by a call for all those between twenty-one and forty-five to report for duty at the local army board. The store closed immediately, and the villagers dispersed in a daze to their homes. Around one in the afternoon, we heard distant explosions from the direction of the Zelva railroad station and understood that bombs were being dropped.

The village was thrown into chaos. People poured out of their houses into the streets, wanting to find out what was going on. The loudspeakers didn't tell us anything. By morning the local authorities could not control the people who were lined up in front of the stores demanding that the managers open the doors. They wanted to buy whatever was available before the Nazis marched into the village. By evening, there was total anarchy, with people looting, sirens screaming, and soldiers running around.

The village officials began fleeing, showing no concern at all for the citizens they were leaving behind. The retreating Red Army was willing to take along young people who were ready to join the war. Some young men did go with the soldiers. Yet even now, in this time of turmoil and danger, Uncle Avrum Chaim showed his faith. As we ran for shelter from the bombs, he expressed his hope that he would survive and be re-united with his wife and child, who were with her family in Sokolow. He hadn't seen them for almost two years; all he had were letters from her forwarded by the Judenrat, a Jewish committee appointed by the Nazis.

The Red Army's image had suffered since we crossed the border; we no longer saw them as invincible. Everyone was shocked at how quickly the Nazis were advancing and how little resistance the Red Army was putting up. Rumors flew that the Soviet leaders had sold out. We refugees were astonished how happy the locals were that the Soviets were retreating. They remembered what had happened in the first world war under the communists, and they expected to be better off under the Germans.

People were fleeing to the forests for shelter from the bombing and artillery fire. As soon as the Soviet troops left, the local Poles took control of Derechin. They donned white armbands inscribed with the word "Militia," placed themselves in charge, and declared their allegiance to the new rulers. Then they began arresting those who had worked for the

Soviets. They also began attacking Jews, looting their homes and demanding, "Give us your gold, your jewelry, your black market currency." They opened the jail doors and released all the prisoners, including the violent criminals the Soviets had locked up. Unable to make sense of any of this, the villagers let the Poles have their way.

When a retreating Red Army regiment stopped in Derechin for two days, we thought we were again under the Soviets. Then on the third day, German paratroops landed nearby, and we knew we would have to hide in the forest. The Nazis were now targeting civilians. People were hiding in basements to avoid being injured or killed by bombs.

About two in the afternoon, we heard orders being shouted for all to leave their hiding places. Assisted by the Poles, the Germans herded the villagers into the courtyard of the Russian Orthodox Church. The Polish militiamen were all local residents and knew the villagers well. Eagerly, they pointed the Jews out to the Germans. During the selection in the church courtyard, the Jews were separated from the rest of the villagers. Those Jews who thought they might escape by pretending to be Gentiles were quickly arrested by the Poles. Jews from nearby Jedwabno were pointed out to the Germans and punished for trying to escape.

Later on, some Jews who had fled Jedwabno for Derechin told us that when the Germans first entered their town, they had herded all the Jews into a barn and set it ablaze. Anyone who tried to get out was cut down by machine-gun fire. Now, standing in lines in the church courtyard, we heard a German tell us in perfect Russian that anyone trying to escape would be shot.

At the selection, a gray-haired, paunchy German captain ordered all professionals—doctors, dentists, nurses, pharmacists, and so on—to step to one side. We tried to delude ourselves that the Germans had suffered many casualties and needed medical staff. A second selection followed, and this time they picked out skilled workers. Next they separated the men from the women, isolating the elderly. We stood in the courtyard, afraid to move, staring at the machine guns trained on us. There was no escape, no hope. Suddenly an artillery shell struck the adjoining building and another struck the church. Confusion broke out. With the Red Army threatening to return, the Germans order everyone to disperse. Within minutes the Germans were retreating toward Zelva.

All through the night, columns of Russian soldiers in tattered uniforms and total disarray dragged their many wounded through Derechin. Obviously they were retreating. The artillery fire continued throughout the night, and no one dared venture out. The whole next day, the Germans rolled into Derechin. The soldiers spread out, parking their horses and wagons. Not wasting any time, the militia announced a curfew from sunset to seven in the morning. Anyone outside after curfew would be risking his life. The Polish militia did what the Germans told them, hunting down Jews, robbing and beating them, injuring and killing many. The next morning the Poles searched the Jewish homes, ordering all Jewish men over twenty to report to the marketplace. At the center of Derechin, ten Jewish men were selected to serve as the Judenrat (committee of Jewish elders).

All around town, the streets were strewn with dead people and horses. The bombed buildings gave the village a weary look. The smoke of fires and the stench of rotting flesh filled the air, adding to the sense of catastrophe. The Jews were more alarmed than anyone else. We had nowhere to turn for safety. We men were assigned to curry the horses and bury the village dead. The Germans buried their own.

The Judenrat was assigned a house. From it they carried out the orders of the Polish militia and the German authorities. Compliance did not lift the danger we faced. From other towns we heard rumors of murders, tortures, and burnings. A message reached us from Ghalinka that passing Germans had massacred all the Jews there.

The violence in Derechin increased daily. When one of the Judenrat members, realizing the futility of his position, asked to be relieved of his post, he was answered with a bullet through the head. Actions like these were carried out in the presence of the assembled Jews, so they would know the power of their tormentors and submit to it without resistance. After a week of occupation, the town was taken over by the Gestapo and the SS. It was now July 1941.

Immediately our new masters herded us to the marketplace for a selection. We had to pass between two rows: the SS on one side, the Polish militia on the other. German officers were seated on a platform draped with swastika banners and Nazi flags. The commandant of the Polish militia, a tall, grim-faced man, introduced the German dignitaries and praised the German liberators, who had saved us from communist oppression. He emphasized his own men's willingness to carry out all the edicts of the Nazi regime. He reminded us again that anyone breaking any new laws would be punished by death.

Then the Gestapo leader rose and declared in a bellowing voice that all the Nuremberg laws would be enforced from now on in Derechin. He ordered the members of the Judenrat to step forward and handed them a list of instructions.

Jews were forbidden to walk on sidewalks. No Jew could come out on market days to buy from farmers. Non-Jews were forbidden to enter the Jewish ghetto. Every Jew—man, woman, child, infant—had to wear at all times a yellow Star of David on the left breast and back. The Judenrat would have to supply the Germans and the Polish militia with working brigades for street cleaning, snow shoveling, house cleaning, and boot polishing. From now on, no Jew could participate in any business. The Judenrat would have to deliver to the Germans 50,000 reichsmarks within twenty-four hours.

We were given twenty-four hours to vacate our houses and apartments and move into the ghetto. We could take with us only the barest necessities: clothing, bedding, and cooking utensils. The ghetto was to consist of three city blocks. At the time there were around four thousand Jews in Derechin, including those who had fled there from smaller communities. Curfew would be strictly enforced, and we would be forbidden to assemble.

At the end of this harangue, we were ordered to hurry home and start moving. Only a few Jews died that day—those who refused to turn over their valuables to the Poles.

For the first time, I saw people mourn the dead without tears. Some expressed envy for those who had died a natural death. All the new orders and fresh abuses had a leveling affect. Derechin Jews and refugees were the same now—all refugees. There was no more elite; we were all suffering the same abuse. What troubled Grandfather Nahum and Rabbi Bakalchuk most was that they would have to shave off their beards.

As instructed, the Judenrat reported to the Gestapo to receive the Nuremberg laws. Its members then went from house to house to explain the new edicts to us. The next day the Judenrat called together an advisory council. Rabbi Bakalchuk was a member of this group. His house was in the ghetto area. My uncle Avrum Chaim had been living there since our arrival, and the rest of our family was able to squeeze into his rooms. Now we all lived together: Grandfather Nahum, our stepgrandmother Golde, Uncle Avrum Chaim, Father's sister Beileh with her husband and child, my two brothers and sister, and me. There was also another family, related to the rabbi. Yet we had plenty of room compared to many. We counted ourselves lucky to be together, close to the news the rabbi brought home from the Judenrat.

Flour rationing began. The Judenrat did not trust the Germans; they feared that the count that was demanded before rationing could begin would be used later for more sinister purposes. So the Judenrat did not forward a true count of Jews to the Gestapo. This was a brave act: our leaders knew quite well they could be shot for such disobedience.

Within a few weeks the ghetto became even more crowded, with more Jews from the nearby hamlets and farms being herded into Derechin. We couldn't hide in the forests; the neighbors and local police were too quick to inform on us. Some of us were sent out in work brigades and were never seen again. The Gestapo would tell the Judenrat to have these men's families send clothing to them, without telling them where. The relatives would pack food and clothes for their loved ones, hoping the packages would reach them.

The "contribution" of 50,000 reichsmarks was only the beginning. Further sums were demanded of the Judenrat. But the committee did not turn over all it collected; it hoped to rescue the Jewish population with these hoarded funds at a later time.

We were organized into labor brigades. Those of us with horses and wagons reported each morning to the Judenrat. Families counted themselves lucky to see their dear ones again in the evening because many on these brigades did not come back. The Gestapo selected its slave laborers with care. Only young and pretty girls were chosen for the jobs of cleaning their headquarters and private homes. Judenrat members who failed to provide workers according to specifications were jailed or mistreated. One of the girls, a striking beauty, was the rabbi's daughter, Esther. She worked at the Gestapo headquarters and turned into a valuable spy, passing on to the Judenrat whatever she heard.

Columns of artillery and cavalry often traveled the main road from Zelva to Slonim. This road, which extended all the way to Moscow, was called the Czar's Highway and had been built by the Russians in the first war. Now Jewish slaves maintained it. Jews with horses and wagons were forced to use them to transport workers. Jews also worked for local farmers and villagers without pay. We sought out this sort of work, for it offered trading opportunities: clothing for food. These assignments also enabled us to stay in contact with people outside the ghetto—a very important consideration.

Jews with certain trades worked in shops that had been established outside the ghetto. These positions, too, were coveted, for they enabled contact with outsiders as well as some protection from the violence meted out on the streets by the militia and the Gestapo. These skilled workers—electricians, carpenters, tailors, cobblers—in turn tried to find jobs for their relatives. They would quickly teach them some secrets of the trade so they could pass as skilled workers. In the shops we could learn when actions were imminent. We would hear a line of trucks roll into town, then hide until the action was over.

Each morning on our way to the Judenrat—we all reported there for our assignments—we had to pass through the cemetery. We often envied the dead who were buried there under their markers. Death was now a friend. We did not fear it; rather we feared the torture of living. Yet the more meaningless life became, the more determined we were to outlive the enemy.

Most Jews cooperated fully with the Judenrat and the advisory board, hoping to preserve lives that way. "Your cooperation may save us all," was the slogan. We wondered why the Poles, who were a minority in Derechin, had been accepted by the Germans and allowed to help administer the town, whereas the Byelorussians, who were the majority and who also opposed the Soviets, were not accepted. It was a mystery.

The most vital question was this: Whose good will should we try to buy in order to save lives? A consensus was reached that we should stay in contact with all our former friends. Rabbi Bakalchuk was well acquainted with the local Catholic and Orthodox clergy. In fact, at the time these churches had been purged, he had intervened on their behalf with the Soviet authorities. Now, in turn, the rabbi asked these clergy to intervene with the Polish militia, to stop the cruel treatment of Jews.

The Judenrat formed a "fishing commando," which delivered its catch every day to the militia and the Germans and sometimes smuggled some fish into the ghetto. A friend of my father, Mr. Weinstock, a member of the Judenrat, got me assigned to this gang—a big favor, for it kept me out of the ghetto, where the work was much harder and the beatings more frequent.

One day, under merciless beatings by the Polish militia, a group of us Jews were made to dig a pit. While we were digging, our tormentors sneered that we were digging our own graves. Yet it turned out that we were digging a grave for our tormentors! We learned later that after the pit was deep enough, the Germans gathered together all our Polish overseers and drove them to the woods, hinting that they were about to take part in a massacre of Jews. The Poles walked to the pit without suspecting anything. There they were cut down by German machine-gun fire, tumbling into the pit before they realized what was happening. In this way the collaboration of Poles and the Germans in Derechin came to an end. It was the rabbi's beautiful daughter Esther who brought us the news that the Polish militia had been annihilated.

7

THE GERMANS NOW ASSIGNED POWER to the Byelorussians. In the fall of 1941 a man named Lewandowski, the post office chief before the war, and a Pole, returned to the village and was appointed mayor. Singling out some wealthy Jews, he had them jailed and demanded ransom from the Judenrat for their release. This was one of the times that the rabbi asked the other churches to intercede.

Derechin was part of Slonim district, so edicts proclaimed in Slonim also applied to us. When contributions were to be delivered from Derechin to Slonim, the Gestapo issued a special travel permit for a Judenrat member; however, this man had to find his own transportation. Because Jews could not keep horses anymore, the Judenrat representative was forced to hire a Gentile to take him to Slonim, paying a premium price.

Jews were forced to hand over all their furs to the Germans. With the freezing cold and record snowfall, we suffered under winter's fury. Also, the demand for labor changed; many brigades now involved outdoor work, which exposed us, ill fed and ill clothed, to winter's storms. Our spirits sank even deeper when in the winter of 1941–42 we learned that the Germans were advancing deeper into Soviet territory. Rumors circulated that the Germans were at the gates of Moscow, Stalingrad, and Leningrad.

There was talk of an impending massacre. We had heard about them in other towns. Word reached us that in Slonim the Germans were killing women, children, and the elderly, along with unskilled workers. The skilled men were spared. There was talk of deportations to places unknown. The Judenrat had to pay for the information it received from Gentiles, so we could never be sure it was accurate.

At this precarious time, Uncle Avrum Chaim's crippled leg became infected, causing him great pain. Accompanied by Aunt Beileh and her husband and child, and with a travel permit obtained through Mr. Weinstock of the Judenrat, we were able to take my uncle to the Jewish

Hospital in Slonim. Aunt Beileh's husband had family in Slonim and would be able to find a place to stay in the ghetto there. The entire family came to say good-bye, wondering sadly whether we would ever see them again. As it turned out, we never did: in the spring of 1942 they were all burned to death in the hospital. The account that reached us told of the SS hurling hand grenades into the hospital to set it ablaze. Any who managed to run out were cut down by machine-gun fire. These were the first fatalities in our family, in the spring of 1942.

I missed Uncle Avrum Chaim very much. He had been a devoted uncle to me and my siblings; he was also a learned man and a spiritual leader, able to find solace in the Bible, which he knew so well. He knew how to raise our spirits and bring us hope, and he helped us in practical ways, too, sharing his food with us. It was a terrible loss for my family, and we mourned him for a long time.

When we first moved into the ghetto, I had helped him build a hiding place over the front porch, constructing a double roof. At the time, we hoped never to have to use it. Soon after, the Germans ordered the Jews to turn in all their sacred books, and they burned them in a bonfire near the main synagogue. But we were able to save an entire set of sacred books and a Torah scroll from the synagogue by hiding them in the double roof. When the ghetto was finally liquidated, this hiding place also saved Uncle Shalom Hirsh and his youngest son from massacre.

One day the Germans found a Torah scroll in the possession of a Jewish family. They executed the entire family as punishment. These were members of my own extended family, who had risked their lives to save the source of our religion, the precious Torah. Those of us who were left decided to move closer together. With so many of us missing, we survivors wanted to be closer so that we could boost one another's morale and help one another however we could.

In my own family there were no longer any adults. Uncle Shalom Hirsh and his family moved into the rabbi's house with my stepgrandmother Golde and me. My brothers and sister continued living next door with Grandfather Nahum, Uncle Moishe, and his child.

The spring of 1942 brought with it a glimmer of hope, even though a big new pit was almost ready. We heard rumors that a German general, von Paulus, had surrendered his army to the Soviets somewhere near Stalingrad. The Jews of Derechin believed that the Soviets would eventually prevail, and in their excitement poured out into the streets in a show of solidarity. But we were still in the ghetto, which was now surrounded by barbed wire fence, and under the wrathful power of the Germans. Fearing that the Nazis would take revenge on us, the Judenrat tried desperately to disperse the crowd, telling all who would listen that such celebrating was premature. The Nazis knew they were losing the war in the east and began directing their anger not just at the Jews, but at the gentile population as well.

Non-Jewish civilians began to suffer along with the Jews. Many were killed, and many others were sent to slave labor camps in Germany. This prompted many young people to flee into the forests, where they formed the core of the resistance movement.

While the Red Army was retreating from the Germans, many soldiers deserted, finding shelter on farms and in villages, among their own people. After the Germans took over, they were required to register with the local authorities, but they were allowed to continue working on farms. These soldiers were glad to have been spared from prison camps.

The Germans started requiring these "easterners" (Russians) to register for work in Germany. To avoid being sent there, some joined the police or the Belarus Guard, which was being trained to fight on the eastern front. But the great majority decided to avoid registration. Fearing they would form an underground resistance, the Gestapo and the local police surrounded villages, rounded up resisters, and shipped them to Germany. To instill fear in others, they also killed many. By now the Germans had assembled special brigades of Lithuanians, Latvians, and Ukrainians, who were even more ruthless than the Nazis, to hunt down and kill Jews.

Many Jews in Derechin had been working outside the ghetto and coming home at night. But that changed: the Judenrat was told that we would no longer work outside. The little food these outside workers had been able to acquire was thus lost to us. With conditions deteriorating, more young people considered fleeing into the forest. This had its drawbacks, however. To start with, the Germans might well retaliate against escapees' families. Also, it would certainly be hard to find shelter. Most villagers and farmers refused to help Jews. Some were afraid of being punished for it; others were Nazi sympathizers and would report any Jews they encountered. For turning in Jewish runaways, the locals were often rewarded with food, a hog, or even a horse.

Meanwhile, the Jews of Derechin were at work digging a large pit and fearing more and more for their lives. The Nazis were demanding new head counts, and beautiful Esther Bakalchuk had more and more trouble eavesdropping on her Gestapo employers so that she could warn the ghetto population in time.

Early one morning, while the work brigades were lining up at the Judenrat, a column of trucks arrived with a roar. Police and SS troops climbed down from them and ordered all Jewish men between eighteen and forty-five to line up on one side. I was in that group. Soon after, Fritz, the head officer of the Gestapo, arrived on horseback, his boots shining in the brilliant sun, whip in hand. In a booming voice he ordered us to run to the marketplace. The rest of the assembled Jews were dismissed. We ran in panic, the SS and police hurrying us on with whips and gunfire. Right after we arrived at the marketplace, we were herded down the road toward Slonim.

We were guarded by a column of SS troops on horseback or on motorcycles, with Fritz in the lead. Trucks filled with police accompanied the column, from time to time replacing the guards running alongside. Any Jew who couldn't keep up was beaten to death by the police or run over by the trucks. I thought this was my end; I could not endure any more beatings and punishment. We all envied the dead, yet our will to live was still there, and succumbing was not an alternative. Losing hope, showing weakness, was a sure death. Slonim was forty kilometers away. Out of 300 men, only 165 got there alive.

On arrival, we were turned over to the Slonim SS and driven like cattle to the city jail. Other prisoners met us there, having been herded from other places. We were finally given some food—a slice of dark bread and a bowl of rye gruel. For three days, we were kept in that jail, sleeping on the bare floors.

At daybreak on the fourth morning, we were marched a few kilometers farther to the railroad yard, where a derailed freight train lay on its side. Cannon shells littered the area, some loose and some still in boxes. Some of us were ordered to collect the loose shells and load them back onto the train; others repaired the rail lines and rebuilt the platforms. We worked from early morning until late evening without food or rest. Many of us did not survive this day of arduous work and cruel beatings.

The next day we were marched toward Lida. Along the way many of us were shot or beaten to death and left on the roadside. We came to a labor camp a few kilometers from Pusewitch, not far from Kozlowshchyzna. Here were three barracks and a kitchen surrounded by a barbed wire fence, with one hut at the entrance for the guards. We would be sleeping on three-tiered wooden bunks. The SS left; our new guards were local police, Red Army deserters, and Poles.

We were to build a road through the forest. Each group coming from the same community was placed in one barrack, with one inmate chosen as foreman. The warnings were the same: if anyone tried to escape, the entire barracks would suffer, and so would our families in the ghetto. From time to time, however, the Judenrat would be permitted to bring extra food or render other help.

After a meal of the same slop as the night before, we were lined up again and marched out to the work site. While marching, I felt ill and vomited. I was sure I was still suffering from the beatings I'd taken on the previous march. I was afraid that if the guard noticed my illness, he would finish me off with a final beating. So I wiped my face and kept up with the rest, holding on to my pain and concealing my suffering. At the construction site we were given picks and shovels. Guards were stationed nearby armed with whips, which they used for any reason or none, as if they were trying to show their supervisors they were worthy of the job.

8

IT WAS MAY 1942. I was almost twenty and generally in good condition, yet between the labor and the beatings, my spirit and body were quickly breaking down. The weather was getting warmer but the soil was still frozen, so digging with shovels was backbreaking labor. The Pole guarding our work brigade was from near Warsaw. One day he started talking to me, trying to explain why he was there. He told me his life depended on pleasing his German overseers. If he dared show any mercy toward the Jews, they would shoot him or send him to a concentration camp. The foreman saw him speaking to me and rushed over to see what we were talking about. The guard explained that he was telling me how to do my job and began beating me to impress his boss. I fainted. The laborers around me left me for dead.

My Polish guard ordered the nearest men to revive me with a bucket of cold water. When I came to, he slipped a piece of bread from his pocket. "Eat it fast and go back to work," he said. "I had to beat you to save your life. We aren't allowed to speak to Jews." My head was reeling, and every part of my body was in agony, but I had to pull myself up and keep working.

After a few days, a delegation from Derechin ghetto arrived with provisions. Instead of food, many of us received soap, thread, and salt. Yet these men were lucky to have received something. As for myself, I received nothing and expected nothing. I knew my family had nothing to send. I was hardly the only one in that situation. The starvation diet motivated me and a couple of my neighbors in the barracks to find ways to exchange the nonfood items for food.

We let the foreman in on our plan. It was a gamble, but we knew that without his support we wouldn't succeed. Besides, he knew he couldn't have stopped us—we were determined to try. In any case, he was as hungry as we were and would be getting his share of whatever we brought back.

Our plan was to dig a hole under the fence, take the nonfood items out, and find farmers who would barter with us. We gathered some barter items from inmates we could trust and planned our "breakout" for ten that night. Confident that we wouldn't dare endanger our families in the ghetto, our guards didn't patrol the perimeter at night. Once the evening count was over, the foreman opened the door to let us out.

The camp was in a wooded area, but the trees closest to the fence had been cleared, obviously to prevent schemes like ours. We dug our escape hole near some small bushes so that we'd have a visible marker to reenter the camp by. Luckily, the terrain was sandy; even so, it took us two hours. We placed the dug-up dirt in some sacks and took the sacks back to camp.

At midnight the sky was clear and the moon shining brightly. We squeezed under the fence, covered the hole with some branches, and made our way toward some barking dogs, hoping to find farms in that direction. Soon we saw the distant light of a hamlet and made our way to a farmhouse on its edge. Not daring to knock on the door, we waited near the barn, hoping the barking would bring someone from the house to investigate.

Sure enough, an old man soon approached and spotted us hiding behind the barn. Seeing that he had no weapon, we went up to him and offered to barter. To our amazement, he thought we were with the Partisans. He told us they had left his house only fifteen minutes earlier. He then asked what we wanted. We were stunned that he might cooperate.

We admitted we weren't from the Underground, but we lied and said that we were from the Slonim ghetto. We apologized for coming at night, explaining that by day it was too dangerous. Realizing his danger, he changed his tune, contending that by helping us he would be endangering himself. We pleaded with him for food in exchange for the items we had brought and tried to pretend we were from a much bigger group that was waiting nearby. We hoped that would give us some protection against treachery.

He went inside to speak to his wife. Five minutes later, both of them came back carrying armfuls of food: bread, cheese, and smoked meat as well as leftovers from their own dinner. They pleaded with us to eat the leftovers quickly and leave their property before anyone spotted us. We ate fast, kissed their hands, and promised we wouldn't return. But please, would he tell us where we could find other isolated farms where we could contact the Underground? The farmer made a sweeping arc with his arm to indicate a large area of farming communities. As to the Underground, we would have to look deep in the forests.

We handed them the barter items. The woman thanked us but did not want any pay—she just urged us to leave and not come back. "Remember," she said, "if we're caught helping you, our lives will be worth nothing." We begged them to take something of our goods—some soap, or salt. The woman finally agreed, though insisting she didn't need them, and pressed us to leave so that the dog would stop barking. We ran for a few hundred yards, so hard our legs grew numb, until we reached the nearby forest. Elated, we started our long trek back to camp. For safety, the three of us divided up the food and kept our distance from each other.

I was the first to arrive back at the fence, happy that we hadn't been missed. The hole was covered with the branches, just as we had left it. I motioned to my companions to bring the earth and spotted our foreman waiting anxiously at the barracks door. I beckoned him to the fence and whispered that we had succeeded. Anxiously, he told us to hurry and helped us cover the hole. We offered some of the food to the foreman and hid the rest. In only a few hours, road building would start again.

In the morning we lined up for head count and were marched to work. But that day the work didn't seem nearly as oppressive. My thoughts were racing with new ideas, new hopes. "Partisans" and "Underground" were new words to think about. How could I join them? What risks would I have to take? How many innocent people might be executed if I fled to them? My mind couldn't rest, with all these thoughts churning.

In the evening, at the stables, my companions, the foreman, and I divided the food we'd brought back and began planning a second expedition. This time we wanted more than food—we also wanted information about the Underground. The following day, one of our trio got sick, but this did not slow us down. The two of us gathered soap and salt for that night's mission. This time our foreman helped us get under the fence.

The moon was full and lit the world with eerie shadows. We ran from the fence with pounding hearts and hid in the bushes for a few minutes' rest while we decided which way to go. We walked for a few kilometers in the direction the farmer had pointed the night before. After ninety minutes we still saw no farms or lights. We began to doubt the farmer's instructions. Was he trying to mislead us? Were we lost? We sat down to rest. Suddenly we heard traffic on the road to Kozlow-shchyzna. In the distance a train was chugging somewhere. This told us to walk in the opposite direction.

A kilometer later we saw a flickering light. At the distant sound of horseback riders, we dove into the underbrush and lay silently listening. We heard fragments of conversations and concluded that the riders were speaking Russian. This was no comfort: many former Russian soldiers were serving the Germans and were as ruthless as the Nazis when they captured Jews. My mind raced; I hoped they were Partisans instead. We stayed in our hideout for ten minutes, our hearts pounding, until the voices faded.

Then we again saw a light in the distance. It was a single farmhouse with a persistent howling dog. As before, we stayed by the barn and waited for someone to come to check on the dog. Soon an old woman came out and began petting the dog, trying to quiet him. But the dog would not stop. At this point, an old man with a limp came to help her. Daringly, we came forward from the barn. We asked them in Russian if anyone else was in the house. They assured us they were alone. We asked them where the Partisans were, but they claimed they didn't know any.

As on the night before, we told them we were part of a larger party looking to exchange soap and salt for food. We asked the woman to stay with us while the old man went for food. The man came out quickly, limping and carrying a bundle of food; the woman offered to go back in the house for more. We gave them the salt and soap, thanked them for their generosity, and hoped we would be able to return for more. They pleaded with us not to risk their lives by returning. They left us with a blessing: "May God save you; we cannot help you."

9

WE BEGAN HEARING that more and more "actions" against Jews were taking place in our district. This news hurt our morale. The delegation from Derechin came again, with food this time, and told us that as long as we kept working on the road, the ghetto would be safe. We felt like hostages; our family ties made escape impossible. The way it was told to us, the hard labor, the starvation, and the beatings were what kept our loved ones alive.

Our Polish guards passed the rumor to us that there were Partisans in the district. The same evening, those guards disappeared. Were they fleeing the Partisans? Or was this a ploy to entice us to escape so that the Nazis would have an excuse for an "action" against us? Our barrack foreman tried to keep everyone in until morning. Our group of three told him that if we heard trucks approaching we would run into the forest through the gap we'd made in the fence. We also shared this information with the rest of the men in our barracks. All night we posted guards to stop anyone from leaving the barracks.

At midnight, figures wrapped in white sheets entered the camp, demanding that we get out or they would set fire to the entire camp. They reprimanded us Jews for remaining in the camp, telling us that as soon as we finished the road, we would be killed. They told us to escape into the forest and join the Underground. We saw Red Army uniforms and automatic weapons peaking out from under the sheets. The sight aroused chaotic feelings in us. We asked them how we could possibly comply with their demands while our loved ones were hostages in the ghettos.

Some younger men were willing to escape and asked how they could join the Underground. Our foreman and my two companions asked one of the men if he could help us, hoping he would tell a small group more readily than the entire camp. But they simply insisted that we leave, and that we stop building the road. To prove they meant business, they set fire to the barrack closest to the entrance. We pleaded with them not to burn the others, at least until morning. That way we would have time to figure out where to go. They listened to our pleas and left the camp.

That night no one slept; all of us were excited by the promise of freedom. We decided to wait until morning to see if the guards returned, then we would decide on further action. The night seemed to drag on forever. No guards returned in the morning. We raided the kitchen and enjoyed one last breakfast without guns and guards. Some men did not wait any longer and simply took off in various directions. We of the Derechin group decided to march back to the ghetto and have the Judenrat solve our dilemma.

While we were marching back, a group of younger men, including me, decided not to return to Derechin to face the Gestapo. Instead we would stay in the forest and find a way to join the Partisans. The older men begged us not to leave them, reminding us what the consequences would be to our families. We replied that the Nazis were untrustworthy but promised we would stay in the forest just that one night, to try to contact the Underground. If we could not find them, we would return to the ghetto.

All night we wandered in the forest, unable to find any Partisans. The villagers were tight-lipped and refused to share any information or help us with food. We had to steal from the fields to keep from starving. The Partisans had vanished like ghosts. After wandering for almost a week in the forest, we decided to return to Derechin.

My family was thrilled to have me back. The conditions in the ghetto were dire, with food harder and harder to find. It wrenched my heart to learn that my good and righteous grandfather Nahum had died. The loss of this kind patriarch, the pillar of our Jewish identity, was immensely painful. Our situation would be even more ominous without him.

Uncle Moishe told me about Grandfather's last days. For weeks, Grandfather had been depressed, withdrawn, and suicidal. Uncle Moishe speculated that his grief at losing my father and his daughter-in-law Sima, and at seeing me shipped to a labor camp, accumulated until it crushed him completely. One morning, at the empty Ark of the Synagogue, now used as living quarters, he prayed with great emotion. Then he yanked out a kitchen knife and began slashing his wrist. A woman in the balcony saw what was happening and began calling for help. People ran up to him and grabbed the knife from him. Suffering minor cuts, he was taken home. Uncle Moishe pleaded with him not to try it again. He tried to remind Grandfather that suicide was a despicable act in the eyes of God.

A few days later, Grandfather told Uncle Moishe that his children and grandchildren needed the food more than he; they needed to survive to carry on the family tradition. As for him, it was time for him to go. The scar on his wrist soon healed, but he was tortured by his transgression against God. He began to decline, his mind and his behavior more and more irrational. Uncle Moishe told my brothers and sister to follow Grandfather Nahum and not let him out of their sight. By the time I returned, he was gone. All that my uncle said was, "God was good to him and took him away."

Before the ghetto was sealed, my brother Chaim Motke had risked his life by venturing out to seek farmers. His efforts to fill my place and provide food for my siblings were remarkable. Chaim Motke was only sixteen. With his blond hair, fair complexion, and gray-blue eyes, he could pass easily as a Gentile when he dressed in peasant clothes. Even so, he was taking a huge risk. Until the ghetto was sealed, he had been able to keep the family on the edge of survival. After it was sealed, Uncle Moishe made him stop these dangerous excursions.

The Germans were intensifying their raids on Jewish homes. To be sick was dangerous, to be young was fatal, to be old was hazardous. The Judenrat tried to help, scattering children through different homes, keeping siblings separated.

My return to the ghetto had huge repercussions. People pointed to me and the other returnees as the reason the Nazis were treating them more severely. Even some family members thought I should have stayed away. Uncle Moishe told me I should have joined the Partisans. "At least one in our family should survive," he said. Then there was the problem of finding shelter for me, a young, able-bodied, unregistered Jew. I was going to have to go into hiding.

Uncle Shalom Hirsh offered to take me back in. I had been living with him before being sent to the labor camp and had helped him build the hideout under the porch roof. I was reluctant to be separated again from my brothers and sister—from Chaim Motke, who had tried so bravely to provide for the children while I was gone; from my little sister, Asna, who was working so hard at being a little mother to her brothers; and from our baby, Yerachmiel, who had been orphaned at such a young age. So I finally agreed, telling myself that if there was an "action," I would be able to hide my siblings with me.

The morale of the people in the ghetto had been shattered. Values had changed; now a good place to hide was the most valuable possession. Only people with valuables left—gold, jewelry, watches—could barter for food. The only currency of any value was the U.S. dollar. People patched their clothes over and over; the dead were buried without clothes, so desperate were the living for them. The digging of the pit continued, and the Derechin Jews well knew they were shoveling their own grave.

Often my Uncle Shalom Hirsh and others would ask me about the Underground. The subject fascinated everyone. The brutality, the beatings, and the horrendous conditions drove me to seek them out. Uncle Moishe approved, and that eased my conscience. My memory of their entering the camp, and their encouraging message, helped me find the courage to try to escape.

Before long, we heard they were infiltrating the Derechin area. There was proof of their presence: Fritz and his entourage of police had been ambushed while raiding a settlement on the Shchara River. One of the police had been killed, and Fritz had been wounded. This news convinced the ghetto residents that the returnees had had a good reason not to remain at the labor camp. The successful ambush of Fritz strengthened my resolve to escape. My head was bursting with problems: Whom could I confide in? Who should break out with me? I decided to approach some boys I had worked with before.

In the morning, while waiting for our work assignment at the Judenrat building, I asked my good friend Yankel Weinstock, whose father was a member of the Judenrat, to help me get reassigned to the bathhouse. The boys at the bathhouse wanted to know about my experience with the Partisans, but I couldn't jeopardize my safety to talk about it. There was one boy in particular, Karpl, whose interest was sincere, and I hoped he would join me in the escape. He knew the area and many farmers around Derechin, and he would have been an asset.

But when he consulted with his family, his mother wouldn't hear of it and angrily demanded that I leave and never come back. She scolded me for trying to drag her son into disaster and warned me that if I tried again she would report me to the Gestapo. No pleading from Karple, who said it should be his own decision, would change her mind. Trying to appease her, I promised not to talk to her son Karple any more. I told her my family was also against it. Another boy's family was just as angry.

Deep in my heart, I was more determined than ever to find a way to fight the Nazi exterminators. My nerves were strained to the limit; I was being lectured every day by someone in my family about my foolish plan.

Then one morning I met Samek Borenstein, who wanted to know how to go about joining the Underground. When I learned that he was the only one left of his family, I asked him if he wanted to escape to the forest with me. His eyes lit up, and I knew he wouldn't hesitate. In fact, he said, he knew others who would join us. For example, there was Hanka, a nurse at the Derechin hospital, who had cared for the Soviet captain Boris Bullat when he had his hand amputated. There also was Leib, who had worked for the Soviets under a false name in the town of Piask. Hanka had heard that Captain Bullat was now a leader in the Underground. I thought Hanka would be a plus to our undertaking. New hope sprung in my heart. Just before curfew, Samek, Hanka, Leib, and I met at the fence to discuss our escape.

That whole day my heart was pounding with excitement and fear. I worried about my siblings and thought of perhaps taking my brother Chaim Motke along. I worried how little Asna and baby brother Yerachmiel Chaim—not even ten years old—would fend for themselves. I was happy to get home and hug my siblings one more time. We ate our meager meal, our last meal together. It was not my own safety that concerned me. How could I justify leaving the children? Was revenge a good enough reason? These questions haunted me.

Uncle Moishe noticed my quivering nerves and took me aside. "Don't worry," he said. "You're making the right decision. I wish I could go with you." He hugged and kissed me, then opened a seam in his jacket and pulled out a U.S. twenty-dollar bill, which he handed to me, urging me to sew it into my clothing. I refused to take it and reminded him that he and the family needed it more, but he insisted I take it: "Who knows, it may save your life." I asked Uncle Moishe not to tell the children, promising that if I succeeded in escaping, I would find a way to let them know where I was. It bothered me that I couldn't say good-bye to Uncle Shalom Hirsh and the family.

When darkness enveloped the ghetto, we met at the fence as planned. Brave young Hanka stood watch, nervously pacing back and forth, while Leib, Samek, and I began digging a hole just under the barbed wire fence big enough to slide under. A narrow canal ran alongside the ghetto, and this we had to cross. One by one we swiftly proceeded, watching to see if anyone had noticed us. As we passed the Derechin hospital, each of us removed the Star of David from our outer clothing. I clutched the army bayonet in my pocket. As the ghetto lights dimmed with distance, our hearts broke in unison at the thought that we were leaving our families.

We walked down the road to Zelva, toward Lipitchanskaia Puszcza (Lipitchanian Forest). In the morning, exhausted from the night's trek, we hid deep in the forest. We lay on the forest floor, the sun casting lacy shadows, the air warm and calm, not a leaf moving. The dry, dark chunks of bread we had brought from home quickly disappeared, barely denting our hunger. Two of us slept while the third sat watch. When night fell we crept out of the forest, searching for familiar farmhouses, some of which I would remember from my time on the fishing brigade.

Three days after we left the ghetto, our food was gone, our stomachs empty. Hidden from the road, we sat by a small fire and baked some potatoes we had dug from the fields. Toward morning we saw a distant farmhouse on the edge of a small patch of forest. Its rundown condition gave us the confidence to approach. We waited in hiding until daylight, watching for any movement at the house. Our young, pretty, blue-eyed Hanka, not very Jewish-looking with her blond braids, was our emissary. A woman would be less menacing to the inhabitants, we judged.

The rest of us waited impatiently until she emerged from the house. She told us she had tried to gather information about the Partisans from the old farmer and his wife by telling them she had lost her way in the forest trying to reach Slizy Podgrobelskie. With night approaching, she was afraid to continue for fear of roaming Partisans. She also told the farmer that she was traveling with family members, who had remained in the forest while she went searching for help.

A while later, she returned to the cottage to try to get some food "for her hungry children." Tensely we waited. We couldn't believe our eyes when she reappeared holding something in her hands. Her bounty included steaming pancakes, fried eggs, sausages, and even a bottle of milk—far more than we had expected.

The farmer had told her how to find Slizy Podgrobelskie, where I had many contacts from the time I worked at the turpentine factory. I hoped those people would remember my fair dealings with them and be helpful now.

10

AFTER TWO WEEKS OF futile wandering, Samek suggested we return to the ghetto for help. Hanka and I said no—better to die in the forest. Yet the farmers who were loyal to the Partisans, and who saw them as their best defense against the Nazis, would not tell us anything about how to find them. So we didn't know how to proceed.

One morning we stumbled into a clearing and saw a farmhouse in the distance. I thought I recognized the place and decided to be the scout. As I entered the yard, a dog growled and bared his teeth. I quickly took shelter, hoping the farmer would come out to investigate. A tall young man with tattooed arms left the house and walked toward me, holding a gun and ordering me to raise my hands and hold still. Shaking with fear, I thought this was my end. He shouted at me to stand still or he'd shoot. Since he hadn't fired at me right away, I guessed that he wasn't a militiaman for the Germans. I told him I was a friend and asked him to call the farmer.

Behind him I spotted the farmer's son, Kolya, approaching. Luckily he remembered me. I asked him to tell this man not to shoot. Kolya assured me I was safe and said I could bring my friends in from the forest. Then he led me toward the farmyard with the other man behind me. The man held the gun in one hand and a grenade in the other. Soon my companions entered the yard and Kolya introduced us to Misha. He told us to relax and enter the house. His father, a cripple, invited us to wash up and make ourselves at home. After we ate, we would talk about everything.

The kind welcome overwhelmed us; it was rare to find a friendly Gentile. My friends and I stared at one another in disbelief. Filled with gratitude, I hugged Kolya and kissed his hands. After washing up, we had our first decent meal in a long time. Noting our fear of the barking dog, Misha went out and put the dog in the barn.

I gathered the courage to ask Kolya why Misha was still holding the gun. "You're safe here," he replied, "so stop asking so many questions." But I had another question: Could he help us contact the Underground? Kolya told me to ask Misha. With laughing eyes, Misha flicked the safety catch on his revolver, dropped it in his pocket, and said: "Well, my friends, let me have the pleasure of introducing myself to you. I am with the Soviet Underground."

Stunned by our good fortune, the four of us fell to our knees, kissing his hands in gratitude. Now Misha began lecturing us: Why weren't the young men from the ghetto escaping to the forests to fight in the Resistance instead of waiting for the Nazis to slaughter them?

How could we explain to him what was happening in the ghetto how the Gentiles among whom we lived all our lives were selling us to the Nazis for a pig or a bag of salt? Gathering my courage, I told Misha that if he helped us, many more would follow us. Misha stared at us for a long moment and then told us he would hide us in the forest until after dark, when his commanding officer was to visit him. He would tell his CO about us, and the CO would decide what to do. We thanked Kolya and his family for their kindness and followed Misha into the forest.

He told us he would whistle three times when he was returning with his commander and cautioned us to stay alert and have one person on guard a few yards away at all times. He warned us that the CO might not come; if not, he would return by himself.

The afternoon and evening dragged on. We were terribly impatient but didn't dare leave the underbrush where Misha had hidden us. Our mood spun back and forth between gloom and hope. Doubts plagued us: Would we be accepted by the Underground? None of us knew how to handle weapons. Misha's tales of raids and ambushes against the Nazis made us wonder whether the commander would consider us worthy. What could we say to persuade him to accept us? We hoped that Hanka, who had nursed Captain Bullat at the Derechin hospital, would be able to influence the commander.

It was almost midnight when three shrill whistles reached our ears. We jumped to our feet and ran in different directions, suddenly confused. The whistle for which we had waited for so long now frightened us. I took a chance, calling out, "Kolya!" But it was Misha who answered. Within seconds, the four of us had gathered around him. Once again he was holding his gun and a grenade.

He greeted us with another lecture: "Never shake hands before you make sure all is safe." He told us he had spoken to the commander, who promised to see us as soon as he could. He offered to take us back to the farmhouse for some food, but we decided to stay in the forest until we knew we had been accepted. Misha said he would return the next day, and this time our signal would be only two whistles.

We had removed the Star of David from our jackets but not from our inner clothes. We didn't intend to return to the ghetto, but we were keeping our stars as symbols of our courage. We would ask the commander to remove them when he accepted us as Partisans. Sprawled on the damp forest earth, I watched the sun rise slowly, sending gentle rays onto my face through the trees. I focused on the glistening dewdrops. I closed my eyes, listening for Misha's whistle, hearing instead the bells of a shepherd's flock. We jumped up when we finally heard the two whistles. Through the rustling foliage we heard Misha approaching. He had come to take us to another good family for breakfast. As we approached this other house, he warned us not to speak to anyone and to answer only when spoken to. Then he introduced us to a farmer, declaring that he, too, was a member of the Underground.

The breakfast was a feast beyond our expectations. We couldn't keep up with the appetites of the others at the table—the portions were too huge for our shrunken stomachs. The four of us had discussed whether it was still necessary for us to eat nonkosher food and concluded that it was more important to stay healthy. Even so, we looked at each other and waited to see who would start.

The farmer had said he would be visiting the Derechin district in a few days, so we asked Misha whether we might send a message to the ghetto. With Misha's permission, we asked the farmer to deliver a message to our friend Karple, whom he knew. We wanted to let our families know we were safe and to learn whether our escape had had any consequences.

After breakfast, Misha led us back to the forest to wait some more for the commander. Hanka told him she had nursed Boris Bullat in the Derechin hospital. Misha hinted that when we joined the Underground, she would be able to meet him. He warned us that the commander was a gruff and serious man but assured us that we needn't fear him. He ran a tight ship and only liked brave men and good fighters. Again, doubts surfaced—there was nothing in our backgrounds to prepare us for this combat. We knew nothing about violence, weapons, and battle. Would that stop us from joining the Partisans?

Around eight that evening Misha announced his approach with the coded whistle. He told us there had been a successful ambush that day. A few Nazis and police had been killed, and they had "liberated" some provisions intended for Derechin. He then led us toward a secluded farmhouse on a hilltop surrounded by a forest. He advised us to show some confidence when we arrived. Outside the well-kept house, a man demanded the password. Misha whistled three times, and we were allowed to come closer.

It amazed us that the guard was wearing a Red Army uniform. Over it he wore a short leather coat. He was armed with a machine gun and wore a belt of grenades. He was small, but the display of all that power made him look like Goliath to us. We followed him into the house, where four men also wearing Red Army uniforms and grenade belts were sitting around a table.

A bottle of vodka stood on the table, and Misha poured himself a drink while introducing us. We were invited to sit down and drink with them, with the comment that a good Partisan knows how to drink. To seem fit for the Underground, we drank. The woman of the house offered to prepare us some food; we refused, not wanting to trouble her.

Within minutes, someone broke out a harmonica and the soldiers and farmers broke out in Soviet songs. We were bewildered that these men could be so brave so deep in Nazi-occupied territory. One of them, a short man with a dark, pockmarked face, crooked nose, and many scars on his forehead beckoned us to follow him into the next room.

"My name is Ivan Zaicev but they call me Vanya," he said. "I heard from Misha that you want to join us." In disbelief, we nodded our heads. He then asked us where our weapons were. When we admitted we had none, he told us that our acceptance depended on finding some; that would show we were ready to fight. Gathering my courage, I asked him how we could get weapons. We would have to raid the homes of some Germans or police and take their weapons from them, he said. That was the only way he knew.

I started reasoning with him that we couldn't possibly succeed in an ambush by ourselves but that we were willing to join one of their ambushes even without weapons, in order to learn from them. After almost an hour, we persuaded him to let us join the Underground on a trial basis. We would go on the next ambush without weapons and try to take them as he suggested. Even this would not guarantee us a permanent place in the Underground, but at least we hadn't been rejected outright.

We returned to the main room, where Vanya called for a toast to the first Jews (to his knowledge) to join the Underground. The farmer asked our names and asked whom we knew in Derechin. He accused us of not being from Derechin because he didn't know us. We could not understand why, after we had supposedly joined the Underground, this farmer was questioning us, but we remembered Misha's instructions and didn't argue.

Vanya was pleased with our conduct, telling us we had passed the first interrogation. Hope again sparked in our hearts. More questioning followed, and when it was over, we had another round of drinks to celebrate the removal of our stars. When we asked Vanya to remove them, he and his companions burst out laughing, but noticing how important it was to us, he ripped the insignias off us, one by one. Once again, we toasted our acceptance to the Partisans.

Soon after this, Vanya took us to the camp. He was glad one of us was a nurse. Hanka mentioned that she had a small cache of first aid items and told him she had cared for Boris Bullat in Derechin. Vanya, a mere infantry lieutenant, worried out loud that Bullat, a man of much higher rank, would "liberate" Hanka into his own unit. He boasted that he had never surrendered to the Germans and that he still had his original uniform and weapons: an automatic pistol, a machine gun, a PPD, and two pineapple grenades. His boot tops were folded like accordions, and he wore an army cap without insignia. He bragged about his knowledge of the forests and told us about his wanderings during his first lonely winter as a resister. He told us he liked good riflemen and hoped we would learn to use all kinds of weapons quickly.

We were nearing Vanya's camp, which was deep in an ancient forest, shielded from sun and rain by towering trees. In the center we saw a hand-dug well framed by a couple of logs, a bucket on a rope attached to a branch for drawing water, a spit over a pit of burning logs, and an iron kettle hanging from crossed branches over the fire for cooking. Only six men were in camp when we arrived. The rest hadn't returned from their latest raid. Vanya pointed to a spot where we could sit down and told us to stay together. We made our lairs under a huge fir tree and finally relaxed enough to fall asleep.

The next morning, one of the Partisans woke us and told us to come get some food. We lined up with the others, stripped to the waist, and washed in the icy well water. As hungry as we were, the sight of fried pork and sausages made us gag. There we were, trying to be like these Gentiles, trying to impress them with our fitness, yet the sight of that food was making our stomachs churn. Even so, we ate heartily, sitting on the ground like the others, not daring to show our disgust.

Vanya introduced us to the other men, who received us in a friendly way. The cook, a tall man with a Ukrainian accent, asked if we liked his cooking. "Of course," we answered. He bragged that his style of cooking was a lot of meat and few potatoes. Was he boasting, or was he trying to heighten our distaste for nonkosher meat? Whatever the case, we told him we liked his cooking a lot. We volunteered to help with the breakfast cleanup. A girl washing dishes pleased him greatly.

After breakfast, we watched the Partisans clean their weapons and prepare their ammunition. We were eager to learn what they were doing, and how. Vanya brought some rusty bullets and showed us how to clean them with sand and wipe them dry with a little oil. He told us we would accompany the group on an ambush in order to secure our own weapons. It would be our chance to overcome our fear of battle and prove our bravery. Having absolutely no training in the use of weapons, we welcomed this chance to participate, protected by the other men.

When Misha came to see how we were faring at the camp, I asked if we could try any weapons. He told us it was forbidden to shoot in camp but promised to take Samek and me some distance away, to practice shooting. Vanya thought this an excellent idea. That afternoon,

Misha, Samek, and I walked from the camp for about a mile. When we stopped, he let us practice breaking down and reassembling a rifle. Then he set up a paper target on a tree and coached us in shooting. He stressed how important it was for a soldier to care for his weapons.

Our first efforts were far off target, and the recoil almost knocked us over, but Misha assured us we would improve. Besides, he said, "it's easier to hit an enemy than a paper target." He praised our first attempts to Vanya, who let us keep practicing.

When the day was over and we returned to camp, we offered to help Kolya prepare the chunks of pork and potatoes for the evening meal. Despite our aversion to the pork stew, we accepted our platefuls. While we were helping Kolya with cleanup, he told us stories of his youth. He was born on a small collective farm near Kharkov and raised in a nursery, where he had little contact with his parents. He grew up in a boarding school, and at seventeen volunteered for the army—a great honor. He attained the rank of sergeant. Just when he was about to continue his education in 1939, Russia liberated Poland, and he was sent to serve in Belarus. In 1941, during the fighting around Derechin, the Nazis offered amnesty to Russian deserters; all they had to do was register for labor camps in Germany. Not eager to serve the Germans, he joined the Underground.

11

FROM THE BEGINNING we joined in the jovial atmosphere of the camp, eager to fit in. Even so, arguments developed, especially when the Gentiles asked, "Why don't more Jews come to the forest to fight?" It was useless to explain the fear we Jews lived with and our lack of weapons. We told them over and over that we were ready to invade the Derechin ghetto with their help and bring out more young men to join the Underground. We assured them that the enemy's strength was minimal and that such a plan could work. They suggested we bring our ideas to the attention of our commander, Vanya.

The camp's weapons expert was a slim, blond, good-natured Partisan with steel caps on his front teeth named Kolka. He told us the password for the night, gave us rifles to practice with, and spelled out for us the first law of the Underground: Every man guards his weapon with his life. "Listen," he said, "think of the rifle as your wife. Be kind to her. In the Underground your weapon is your sweetheart and your head, and no one wants to lose either."

Samek and I often spoke about the kindness and courtesy of Kolya the cook and Kolka the weapons expert. How extraordinary it was for a Ukrainian and a Georgian to show acceptance and kindness toward Jews!

That night I couldn't fall asleep. The words kept echoing in my mind: "A wife without a wedding, and a sweetheart without love." I considered my position. Yeshaye Hershel, son of Itzche Meier, grandson of pious Grandfather Yidl and pure-of-thought Grandfather Nuhim, a Partisan, safe in the woods, while back in Derechin my brothers Chaim Motke and Yerachmiel Chaim and my little sister, Asna, and my uncles, aunts, and relatives were suffering under the Nazis' bestial cruelty. I searched within myself for the strength to be brave. In the dim, distant light of the smoldering campfire, I practiced breaking down and reassembling a rifle, while my mind conjured up the ghetto, the Gestapo, and the militia. I saw myself fighting the Germans, running and shooting, taking revenge till the last bullet.

As the first rays of sun penetrated the crowns of the trees, the Partisans returned from their night's work. We heard the clang of two frying pans, a signal that breakfast was ready. Kolya showed us how to flip pancakes in the air.

Some of the faces that morning were new to us. Kolya turned to one of them and said, "Commander Vasya, these are our four new members. They're from the Derechin ghetto."

"I'm Vasily Pishchulin," the man said. "They call me Vasya." He was a tall, broad-shouldered man with a mane of blond hair crowning a low forehead. When he smiled, two gold crowns shimmered. "You are brave not to have waited for the Nazis to kill you," he told us, "but to have joined us instead."

Kolya whispered to me that it was Vasya to whom we should present our plan to raid Derechin. Noting Vasya's interest, we told him all we knew about the defenses in and around Derechin, and how many police and Germans were on guard there. We insisted that the police and the Gestapo hadn't installed any bunkers yet. We emphasized that the ghetto's young people knew well that they couldn't help their families and would eagerly join the Underground.

Vasya listened carefully and then told us that an attack like the one we were suggesting required thorough preparation. He told us he knew all about the activities of the Nazis and would present the plan to Boris Bullat, commander of the General Staff. Excited by this information, we told him that Hanka was a nurse and knew Commander Bullat, having cared for him at the Derechin hospital.

Before the day was over, Vasya took me out for rifle practice. He introduced me to the Russian machine gun, the PPD. I was eager to join a raid on Derechin. I fantasized about capturing a policeman and listening to him beg for mercy. I saw myself pointing a rifle at his head, holding his life in my hands, taking revenge for the suffering of my family. Immersed in this fantasy, I appealed to Vasya to include me in a raid. He asked me if I could climb trees. And did I know how to use field glasses? I told him I would show him I could. That evening, he told us we could join him in the next raid, which was being planned for the weekend.

Our camp had three observation posts. Two men were assigned to each. One perched in a tree while his partner stood guard nearby. When the man up the tree saw someone approaching, the man on the ground would run to relay the information to the next post, which in turn would relay it to the commander in charge, who would then get the message through to the camp commander.

After he trusted me to stand lookout, Vasya assigned me a place in the next ambush, which would take place on the road between Derechin and Volia, a large village. The police were going to take that road to arrest some Russian dissenters who were refusing to report for the labor battalions that were being sent to Germany.

On our way to set the ambush, I was heartened by the relaxed manner of my Partisan comrades. They showed no fear or caution, and laughed and joked as if we were in complete control of the area. I could hardly believe I was part of this group.

We stopped to rest, and Vasya asked me why I wasn't laughing like the others. Was I scared? I smiled and assured him I wasn't. Yet deep in my heart, I understood how momentous this mission was: I was about to become a killer. What would that mean to my adherence to Jewish laws as taught to me by my grandfathers Nuhim and Yidl?

It was May, the season in Russia when the forest wakes from her winter sleep. The trees were growing back their thick foliage, caressed by the penetrating sun. The fields were alive with wheat and corn, stalks swaying in the gentle breeze. We had been in the woods for several weeks. After walking for an hour, Vasya gathered us together to review our plan.

With Alyosha, a local Byelorussian, I was to climb a tree and watch for the enemy. Two other men were to form the ground patrol. The remaining six of us, armed with a single air-cooled machine gun, one ten-shot recoilless rifle, and a personal PPD each, dug in on both sides of the road. Each man also carried a pistol. Only the men on the ground had hand grenades—two each. Vasya carried his PPD with two back-up ammunition clips, and a pistol and two hand grenades on his belt. The three men on the left side of the road were to open fire after our targets passed. We would attack with grenades and follow up with machine-gun fire. If the enemy took cover on the opposite side of the road, our second group was to open fire to keep them pinned. I was to come down from the tree to report the number of enemy and what weapons they were carrying. Alyosha was to stay in his tree to watch for reinforcements. No one was to retreat unless ordered to do so, or until the last bullet was gone. If we did retreat, each man would have to return to the camp on his own.

Vasya told us that according to his information, there were only ten men in the convoy, either police alone or police and Germans. If there were more than that, we wouldn't engage them. Were there any questions? No? "Then good luck, comrades."

Trying hard to look calm, but trembling all over and with my stomach in knots, I marched with the others to the ambush position. Now Vasya showed us where to place ourselves and how to camouflage the machine gun, and told us to be ready to fire. He asked me how far I could see with the field glasses, to point out the object. He climbed the tree and took the glasses from me. Surveying the area, he specified the exact distance at which I was to sight the enemy and when to come down to join the men on the left side of the road. With all my heart I prayed to God for the courage and strength to carry out my assignment.

Then Vasya positioned the second group, with Alyosha in the tree. Once the runners were at their posts, Vasya positioned himself with the first group, on my side of the road. I was relieved to see him there. It was ten in the morning.

Twenty minutes later I spotted a man galloping a horse straight toward our position. I called Sergey, my runner, and told him what I saw. He immediately informed Vasya, who ordered him to stop the rider and find out why he was galloping his horse. Sergey waited for the man to get a little closer, then stepped into the road and waved the rider to stop. By then Vasya had recognized the rider as an informant for the Underground. He told us a column of Germans and police were coming our way, then continued down the road toward Volia to alert the settlements along the way.

Now Vasya came over and stood below my perch to give me more instructions. There would be policemen riding bicycles and a carriage, he said. When they came into view at the marker he had picked out, I was to come down and with my runner, Sergey, rush to our assigned position on the ground.

Terrified, I prayed again for courage. Straining my eyes, not daring to blink, I watched for the black-uniformed policemen—"the Black Crows," we called them. Visibility was excellent that day. Finally I saw in the distance several men on bicycles. Soon I could discern two lines of bicycle riders, one on either side of two carriages.

Shaking like a leaf, I wasn't sure any more of the marker, so I scrambled down from the tree and followed Sergey to our position on the roadside. We waited for the bicycles and carriages to pass our position and for the signal grenade to go off.

One of our men, Sasha, a tall, slim Russian, stepped from his hideout, leaned against a tall pine tree, and tossed a grenade into the first carriage of Germans. A shower of machine-gun fire followed the explosion. The second carriage came to a halt a little distance away. The police and Germans took cover on the opposite side of the road from our position and started to fire back. The horses were killed instantly. Our group on the opposite side let the Germans and the police take positions. When the surviving Germans and police began firing, our side fired back with all the weapons we possessed. At the same time, we began shouting for our targets to surrender.

Almost immediately, a German began waving a white handkerchief and shouting for his men to cease fire. I had ten bullets left when the shooting stopped. Along with Sergey and the others, I came out onto the road. Our machine gunners kept us covered. In a commanding voice, Vasya yelled to the German in charge for his men throw their weapons down on the road. In Russian he warned the police not to play any tricks—one shot and we would mow them all down. One by one, like whipped dogs, they came out, threw their weapons onto the road, and raised their hands.

Euphoria took hold of me. Among our prisoners I recognized policemen and Germans from the ghetto. The group's commander was a first lieutenant in the *Sonderkommando*. I asked him in German how many were in his group. He answered that there were two German officers and ten police. We counted five dead or wounded, one escaped policeman, and four prisoners—one German and three policemen.

Vasya ordered us to put the wounded out of their misery. It was a rule in the Underground not to take any wounded prisoners. He chose Alyosha, Sergey, and me as the executioners. I couldn't decide if it was a duty or a pleasure. We left them in the brush. I realized then that it was not my pleasure. It tormented me, the ease with which we held life and death in our hands. I was learning that I wasn't a cold-blooded killer. My conscience bothered me, but there was no time to think about it right then.

Vasya ordered the carriages and bicycles burned. Then we gathered up the captured weapons and ammunition and marched the prisoners to our camp. My determination to take revenge vanished in the wind. How could I kill so effortlessly? It was almost like I was becoming two different people: Grysha the Partisan, an Underground fighter, and Hershel the gentle and devout Jew. I could still hear the voice of one wounded policeman begging us for his life. Like a maniac I had shouted at him, "How many Jews have you killed? Did you pity them when they pleaded for their lives?" Biting my tongue and struggling to hold back my nausea, I followed the Partisans.

Vasya dispatched two men to a farm to borrow a horse and wagon for transporting our captured arsenal to camp. About a mile before our first lookout post, he instructed us to unload the wagon and send the farmer back home. Among the weapons we had captured were two German pistols. I asked Vasya if I could keep the pistol and holster I had removed from the dead officer. He grinned and said, "Keep it—a souvenir of your first ambush." I thanked him and immediately strapped on the holster and pistol. The weight on my hip made me feel invincible, a real man, as if I had been with the Underground all my life.

The Partisans stripped the boots off the prisoners' feet and made them trek barefoot through the twigs and pebbles of the forest floor—a deterrent to running away.

My first ambush had been profitable. Besides gaining fighting experience, I had a "liberated" pistol in a holster, new boots, and a pair of pants (from one of the dead policemen). I had also acquired self-confidence and proved myself to my comrades.

Along the way, I questioned the German lieutenant about the fate of the Jews in Derechin. He was reluctant to tell me. Vanya stepped in and ordered him to cooperate or else. His voice trembling, the German disclosed that he didn't know how much longer the ghetto would remain because Berlin was calling for a "final solution to the Jewish question in the whole of Belarus." The term "final solution" was new to me, and I didn't know then what it meant.

Vasya ordered me to stop asking about the ghetto and to grill the officer for the names of informers near our camp. The German refused to tell me. Following Vasya's example, I told him his life might depend on his cooperation, so he relented and named two men. One lived in Slizy Podgrobelskie, the other in Volia, the Underground's backyard. This information was important, though it seemed meaningless at the time because I was tortured by thoughts of the ghetto.

When we returned to camp, I wondered why we had brought the prisoners back. I imagined them escaping and returning with reinforcements. It amazed me that my new comrades had come to trust me so quickly.

The other Partisan groups in the area quickly learned all about our ambush. Other commanders congratulated us on our success. Local farmers acted as messengers between our groups. Unfortunately, the Germans used the same farmers to spy on us. Many contacts worked for both sides, so neither side could ever be sure it was receiving reliable information. Both sides walked into traps. Those with dual loyalties lived their lives on the edge, not knowing which side would get them.

Back in camp, we received a hero's welcome from Vanya and Misha. In the afternoon Boris Bullat, the one-handed commander we had waited so long to meet, approved our acceptance into Vanya's group. Hanka, who knew Bullat from the Derechin hospital, was transferred to the field hospital, where she could be of more use.

We celebrated our success with food, song, and vodka. Vasya and his group were applauded as the heroes of the day. The prisoners were questioned by our commanders, then shot. The guards were allowed to keep the prisoners' clothing. The commanders kept only the black uniforms of the police. We used these uniforms to impersonate Black Crows when we went hunting Nazis and their collaborators. The latter were rounded up and shot, their farms confiscated by the Underground. One time, the Underground ordered a farmer known to be a collaborator to load onto a wagon the dead bodies from an ambush and take them to the Gestapo in Derechin.

12

THE UNDERGROUND WAS STARTED by Soviet soldiers who found themselves caught behind enemy lines during the German invasion. To avoid being "drafted" into labor battalions in Germany, many of them hid on farms, where they worked clandestinely just for their keep. Some farmers, being shorthanded, were glad of the free labor; others happily turned in these illegals in return for some reward from the Germans; still others handed over their own soldiers reluctantly, only so that they wouldn't be killed for harboring them. Many farmers helped the Soviet soldiers for only a while, until fear overwhelmed them. To avoid being captured and killed by the invaders, many soldiers fled to the forests, where they formed small bands and survived by raiding farming collectives for food and weapons.

When I first joined the Underground, the local organization was independent—it wasn't guided by or linked to the larger force, which was controlled by Moscow. In those days, the early summer of 1942, our group had little contact with the much larger and stronger units operating around Nalibokie and Vilna. We were strictly a local band operating around Slonim, Zdiatlovo, Novogrodek, Lida, and Derechin—roughly one hundred square miles. We hid in the forests and lived by our wits and guns.

In our camp we met Pavel Bullak, a slender, blue-eyed man with a birthmark on one eyelid and a wisp of blond hair hanging over the other. He was a farmer in the village of Ostrow near Derechin. He had been installed as a village elder by the Soviets during their occupation of Belarus. When the Russians retreated, Bullak stayed put. When the Germans invaded, he escaped to the forest, where he gathered a group of men from his village to fight the Germans.

The rumor among the local farmers was that Bullak had retreated with the Soviets to Russia. Actually, he and his men were fighting by day in the Underground and going home to their wives and families in the village at night. They depended on the locals for help, information, and food for their families. They collected supplies for themselves by raiding farms in other districts where they wouldn't be recognized.

Bullak was an accomplished warrior and famous as a quick draw. He carried his PPD like a necklace and was always ready to use it. His reputation for bravery was spreading, and to many Partisans he was a legend. Soon enough, his fame reached the Nazis, who offered a large reward for him, dead or alive. It amazed us four Jews that small groups of Partisans could survive right under the noses of the Germans. I was in awe when I met Bullak, and gratified to hear there was a Jew in his group. I was thrilled when I learned that other Derechin Jews besides us four had succeeded in joining the Underground. After the Derechin massacre, they joined Bullak's *otriad* (company).

When the High Command visited our camp, Samek and I mustered the courage to propose an attack on Derechin. That command included the leaders we already knew about—Bullat, Bullak, Komorov, Vanya, and Vasya. We were deeply disappointed when they told us the attack we were suggesting could not be launched at that time.

The next morning, after the High Command left, Vanya assigned new weapons to all of us. Now, besides my pistol, I had a ten-shot recoilless rifle. Samek and Leib were handed Russian carbines. Hanka had been assigned to another camp, where she would help organize an infirmary. It was a sad parting, but we knew we had no say in the matter.

The fact that an infirmary was being established was an indication that the Underground was digging in. It would be in a secret place; only a few knew exactly where. We learned soon enough that what our friend Misha had told us in the very beginning applied here as well—don't ask too many questions. In the Underground, order and military discipline were strict.

The German-backed police and their administrative puppets were taxing the farmers heavily by tithing their crops. The farmers were, in effect, slaves of the Germans. The original Underground groups didn't concern themselves much with the farmers' hardships, but eventually that would change.

The Nazis' propaganda had declared us a puny gang of renegades and bandits. At the time, most of the German forces in Belarus were busy fighting on the eastern front, which actually helped us by giving us breathing space to organize. Our skirmishing was keeping the Nazis busy, delaying their actions against the Jews in the ghettos, in effect providing a temporary reprieve. However, when the Germans found that they couldn't simultaneously fight us and terrorize the ghettos, they speeded up their liquidations of the Jews in the smaller towns.

The local people, mostly farmers, were tired of the Underground being controlled by Soviets. Many of them remembered the Soviet occupation, the oppression, the confiscation of their farms, and the deportations of entire families to Siberia. Many hated communism but hated the Nazis too, for ruthlessly enforcing total submission. Many of the farmers who helped us were simply being practical—it was easier to appease us than the Nazis. That is, they gave up less by siding with us. But all of this meant that our district was ravaged by the Germans in the day and stripped by the Underground at night.

The forest was our home. Any civilians we caught wandering in the forest were closely interrogated. We established couriers as well as regular contacts in each area, including the Nazi-occupied towns. Some of these contacts were also German collaborators. The Germans had an extensive network of spies and informers. Those who were cooperating with us were doing so for selfish reasons, for the safety of their families. But there were also some idealists who believed in communism and wanted it to return.

Sometimes we persuaded local farmers to side with us by rescuing their farms from Nazi collaborators. Also, anyone who betrayed one of our contacts to the Nazis was executed without hesitation. After our region became organized under one command, we established other policies as well, though always with the same end—victory over the invaders. The Nazis responded to all of this with heavier weapons and more troops.

The Underground began using horses for operations requiring contact with distant settlements. Information was useful only if it was quick. Four legs were faster than two and could penetrate the forests more easily. Each group in our area began patrolling regularly on horseback.

I began to feel a strong allegiance toward these forest men. The primitive life, the struggle to survive, and the desire to win all contributed to the camaraderie. We felt responsible for one another just as much as for ourselves.

It moved me deeply that Vanya trusted the Jews in his group. He shared information about his attacks with us and discussed our assignments openly. This trust underscored our acceptance and made us feel at home. We were told about the strength and the power of the police stations and the defenses they possessed. On raids and ambushes, each member of our group always knew exactly what was expected of him. It was around this time that I learned the motto of the Underground: "We don't surrender. The last bullet is for oneself."

"We don't surrender." That simple sentence made me shiver. So did this declaration of our commanders: "Our only goal is to fight the Nazi scourge."

I marveled at how relaxed my comrades could be. In the heart of enemy territory, they would walk right into a village looking for a party. "Drink, dance, make love, and be merry"—that was their motto. It astonished me that my comrades could forget so easily the dangers they faced.

Not long after I joined, a General Staff and Supreme Command were organized. Until then, we had known the Supreme Command only of our own Lipitchanian Forest groups. The commanders of Nalibokie Forest now joined forces with us, and the entire region was placed under the command of an officer named Senitchkin. Each group was identified by the name of its commander, and all these commanders began meeting once or twice a week. Each group was assigned a certain district as its territory. Boris Bullat, the man we had waited so long to meet, was voted leader of the Lipitchanian Forest group. Every *otriad* was given the name of a Soviet hero. Bullak, the quick draw, was a subordinate of Bullat and commanded his old group.

Once this new arrangement was established, each group was told to stage an ambush to show the Germans we meant business in our district. Then each group was to eliminate a local police station. Each of these stations was manned by ten to fifteen police. Because these stations had no heavy weapons, they were never strengthened by bunkers or other strongholds.

Our group was assigned to attack a police station near Ghalinka on the road between Derechin and Slonim. All telephone lines were to be cut. So that all fighting men would be free for the attack itself, we sometimes enlisted farmers for noncombat tasks like cutting wires or burning wooden bridges to hinder the target's escape or the arrival of reinforcements. In raids such as the one we had been assigned, each Underground group was supported by a backup unit in case a retreat was necessary; there was also a third unit to set up ambushes along the approaches to the police station.

We were to surround the station, open fire, and demand a surrender. If the police fought back for too long, we were to set fire to the station if possible and then retreat. We were to attack at four in the morning, when the police station was at its least alert, with most of the men asleep.

All groups involved left their camps at nightfall. We were under strict orders not to stop at any farm or leave the group for any reason. We were given a specific place to meet. When we got there, the commanders would separate us into bands of three or four and assign us our positions. When we heard a hand grenade explode, that would be the signal for the attack.

The moonless night was perfect for our purposes. Black clouds told us rain was coming. A predetermined password was whispered from ear to ear; it was to be used only to signal a retreat. Half an hour before four, we were all in position and waiting for the signal.

Ghalinka was a farming village in flat terrain, surrounded by bush and fields of rye and wheat. Walking was easy, the crops tall enough to hide our approach even by day. Nearby, off the main road, stood a well-kept two-story farmhouse—the police station. It was surrounded by a tall wooden fence and had an gate wide enough for a truck. The single guard stationed outside was to be eliminated immediately.

I had already been through an ambush, but this was an attack, so the tactics were new to me, and I was terrified. I tried to push my fears out of my mind and scanned the area in front of me. Would we succeed? Would I have the courage to do my job and meet the expectations placed on me? I remembered that Nazi paratroopers had murdered all the Jews in Ghalinka and felt more determined than ever to succeed. Now that I had a gun in my hand, I owed it to the martyrs to take revenge.

Then the grenade exploded, and like a herd of wild animals, we bellowed "Hurrah!" and stormed the station yard. We had caught the police off guard, literally napping, so they put up almost no resistance. We captured the building while our backup groups harnessed the horses and began loading ammunition and supplies onto the wagons.

A number of police were killed. Those who surrendered we marched back to camp. While we were loading the wagons, some of us made what we called a "bombing"—that is, we began robbing the local people of their clothing, food, and moonshine. For revenge, some of us killed the families of the policemen and razed their houses. As I watched, I wondered: Were we fighting Nazis? Or were we getting revenge? Or were we just a horde, out of control and enjoying ourselves while we could?

Dawn was breaking when we reached our camp again. The chimneys of the farmhouses we passed were puffing smoke, and the aroma of *blini* (yeast pancakes) filled the air. Farmers met us along the path, commenting about our resistance. Some asked, "What are you up to, now, boys? You know you're only inviting trouble onto our heads." Others, hearing that our raid had succeeded, praised us as heroes. Some wanted to know the fate of certain policemen who were especially brutal and rejoiced that they wouldn't be harassing them anymore. The attack on Ghalinka must have made an impact among the local farmers, for in the weeks to come more of them joined the Underground.

Many were astonished that Samek and I, Jews, were among the Partisans. Many made insulting remarks about us. I didn't understand why our commander had decided to tell these people we were Jews. I asked Vanya and Vasya about it, and they explained that they were trying to get the information relayed by the rumor mill to the Derechin ghetto. The point was to let the police know that by setting foot on our territory they would be risking their lives. We hoped this information would help keep the police at bay. Yet we couldn't help wondering if the Nazis would retaliate against the Derechin ghetto when they found out there were Jews among the Partisans.

Most of the Partisans drank an amazing amount of alcohol. If attacked during a binge, there was no way they would be able to put up a decent fight. I abhorred this behavior; they were risking everything they were fighting for, for the sake of a moment's pleasure, and the commanders didn't just allow it—they joined in it. This lack of responsibility alarmed me. Yet it seemed typical of the Russian character. If we won an attack, there was reason to celebrate, so they drank; if we were defeated, they needed to drown their sadness in drink.

We rested for a while after returning from the Ghalinka raid. Then we went to visit the local farmers, those who sympathized with us, to celebrate our victory. For the first time, Vasya asked me to go along. I hesitated but went with them in the end, to prove I belonged. There was dancing to accordion music, and, of course, the vodka was flowing. Yet I could not savor our victory with the rest; I was constantly thinking about my family and fellow Jews in the Derechin ghetto.

Weary of drawing attention to my mood, I pretended to be drunk. The sarcastic jokes about Jews not being able to hold their liquor made me more and more apprehensive, and I began to realize I would never be seen as an equal. But I also knew I couldn't change that, so I let them have their fun at my expense. Finally, Vasya called his boys to order and told them to leave me alone.

But I still wanted to prove myself, so I asked for another drink. They asked me to dance, and when they saw I could still stand upright, they seemed pleased. They even cheered me on: "The Jew can hold his liquor!" Daylight was breaking when the party broke up and we trudged back to camp.

Only with Samek could I share my feelings. The ghetto was never far from our thoughts. We were anxious to get a message into the ghetto, to urge more boys to escape. Misha, our original contact, was away from camp most of the time, acting as a liaison with the nearby communities. One of his contacts was Kolya, in whose house we had met Misha. We asked Misha to let us go with him so we could talk to Kolya. We wanted to send another message to the people in the ghetto. Sensing our distress, he agreed to take us along.

It was now June 1942; the weather in the forest was pleasant. The days were warm and sunny, the nights cool and congenial. But not all was well. Our camp was in a low valley swarming with mosquitoes, and there was no escape from them. Our nights became nightmares— we were being eaten alive.

A few days later, true to his word, Misha took Samek and me along to see Kolya. Along the way he told us about his travels and how he collected information. He stopped at a friend's house. Before approaching it, he explained that in the Underground one never goes anywhere without checking whether the coast is clear. Also, even if we were armed, it was dangerous for everyone to enter a house at the same time. Then he told us how to place a sentry before entering a building. He emphasized how important it was never to panic. We listened carefully to all his advice and promised ourselves to emulate his caution.

Misha entered first while Samek and I stayed outside. If there was trouble he would fire one shot in the air and Samek and I would split up and cover him at the exit. But soon he came out and told us to enter and have some food while the farmer stood guard outside. We wondered if it was safe to leave the farmer as a guard. Reading our minds, Misha smiled and said, "Don't worry, comrades, our man out there has a gun in his pocket, and if there's trouble, he might have to run with us. So come in and make yourselves comfortable."

There was food and drink in abundance. This farmer was the man we had asked to get a message to the ghetto many days before. Anxiously, we waited for him to tell us what he knew. We were crestfallen when he told us the police now patrolled the ghetto and it was harder even to get near the fence to speak to anyone. He added that some farmers who had tried to speak to the Jews had been arrested. We feared that Derechin was about to be destroyed.

When we came to the farm that was our destination, we heard from Kolya that the locals were very happy with the Underground for having destroyed the police station. He told us that the following day the Germans had come from Slonim and reorganized the station, arming their men to the hilt and establishing a number of precautions, including a curfew in the area. We would have to be especially careful when going back to camp. The police had been ordered to move their own families to the towns where they were serving; also, unmarried police were not allowed to go home or visit friends. He also told us that the Derechin garrison was being reinforced.

Samek and I were worried about the new rules in the ghetto. Misha, trying to cheer us up, suggested another drink. We asked Kolya to keep in touch with us and let us know what was happening in Derechin.

13

ONLY THREE DAYS AFTER OUR TALK with Kolya, and three months after our own escape, Derechin ghetto was liquidated. From some of our supporters in the countryside and from the survivors who escaped to our forest, we learned about the horrors that the Nazis perpetrated that day.

Fearing the Partisans, the Germans had moved against the ghetto more quickly than they might have. The day before the liquidation, the Judenrat had been summoned to Gestapo headquarters, where they were brutally beaten and ordered to deliver a big monetary contribution as ransom. The members of the Judenrat went door-to-door collecting funds to be delivered to the Gestapo. Desperately the people tried to scrape together the outrageous amount demanded in money, gold, and clothing. By evening the ransom had been delivered.

My mother, Sara, holding my younger brother, Yerachmiel. I am next to him on the right. My sister, Asna Gitel, and my brother Chaim Motke are in the bottom row. This picture was taken in Ostrolenka in 1935.

This picture was taken at the wedding of my father's sister and includes my father, mother, four of us children, my grandfather on my father's side, my father's three sisters, and his brother. I am the only survivor among those pictured.

A wedding in Ostrolenka, 1937. The bearded ones are the Cukierman brothers.

Former partisans who fought in various forests in Belarus. I was working in the camp administration. The photograph portrays the transportation of youngsters to a special *aliya* camp; I am first from the right in shorts. October 8, 1945, in Modena, Italy.

Various partisans in Modena, Italy, in 1945. I am standing on the left.

This picture of me was taken after my arrival in Modena, Italy, in May 1945.

At the camp in Modena, Italy. I am at the speakers' table conducting the gathering.

My daughter, Rosalie; son, Michael; wife, Sonia; and me at Michael's bar mitzvah.

My family in Chicago, 1980.

Next the Judenrat was ordered to provide the Gestapo with a fresh list of people in the ghetto. Based on this list, new certificates were issued called "life certificates." The Judenrat was told to distribute these certificates the next morning to people they considered vital to the ghetto's operations. People without these papers would have to register with the Gestapo for work papers.

There was bedlam when this information reached the Jews, who deduced very quickly that without a certificate they were doomed. Even those *with* certificates didn't trust the Germans, and many went into hiding or fled to the forests.

In the night, the local police surrounded the ghetto. At sunrise, trucks filled with SS troops drove into the ghetto to reinforce the Gestapo. The Judenrat was ordered to assemble the men with the special certificates. The Gestapo loaded them onto trucks near the ghetto entrance and drove them to the marketplace, deluding them by creating the impression that they were being selected for a work brigade.

In the weeks and months before, the Jews had been forced to dig a pit in the forest. It had been assumed that this would be the last resting place of the Derechin Jews. But it wasn't. On that infamous day, the Jews who had assembled in the marketplace, and others drafted from their hiding places, were driven like cattle toward the craters created by the German bombing of Derechin. There, forlorn, confused, helpless, they were slaughtered and thrown into the craters. While Nazi troops, aided by Ukrainian and Lithuanian police, were shooting unarmed Jewish men, women, and children, Derechin ghetto was being burned to the ground. It was July 24, 1942.

In this way, in just one day, the Jews of Derechin vanished from the earth. Over three thousand Jews had lived there. For generations they had worked, studied, produced wise men and scholars, and suffered yet flourished. In one day all had perished, murdered by a vicious enemy.

A handful of survivors somehow escaped the inferno. Wandering in the woods, alone, hungry, frightened, and cold, some of them arrived at our camp. They were shadows of men—confused, disoriented, and in shock. Hoping for a miracle, I begged them for news of my family. Joy filled my heart when I learned that Uncle Shalom Hirsh and his little son, Akiva, had somehow escaped. There were others I knew among the survivors; Mr. Weinstock's daughter Rivkele and his sister-in-law were two. I mourned for the boys who had worked with me on the ghetto bathhouse. Why hadn't they listened to me at the time and followed me into the forest? They could have lived!

Later, Uncle Shalom Hirsh told me that he and his son had survived by hiding in the false roof I had helped build into the porch. The rest of the family never had a chance to reach that shelter. Peeking through a crack, he had watched the ghetto residents, including my siblings, being rounded up and shot. He had watched the murderers torturing their victims before killing them. My heart broken, I cried at the fate of my brothers and sister and the rest of my family who had perished.

When Uncle Shalom Hirsh saw me dressed in a Red Army uniform, a pistol on my hip, an automatic rifle slung over my shoulder, he hugged me and with bitter tears demanded: "Why didn't they listen to you when you told them to escape to the Underground?" Consumed with grief, he lamented his own fate. Only the will to save his little son drove him to escape the Nazi butchers.

The sight of these terrified survivors, their accounts of the horrors they had seen, the faces of the terrified young children, made me determined to harden my heart, to check my emotions, to never forget the innocent blood shed by the Nazis and their collaborators. I vowed to fight the enemy without mercy and to the bitter end. No longer fearing death, I swore a private oath to take revenge.

The Underground had a new problem—how to care for children, women, and old people. Vanya's group, which was our unit, immediately set up a relief kitchen, creating a "family camp." Really there were no families; not even one entire family had survived. The only larger family group was the Lipshovitzes, three brothers and a sister. They reassembled in the forest, where they turned themselves into courageous Partisan warriors. The three brothers survived till war's end; the sister died heroically, one of the few warrior women at Slizy Podgrobelskie.

One brother, a member of a Zionist group, was killed after the war by a member of the Armia Krayowa (The National Army) in the Polish city of Lodz.

Vanya and Vasya assigned me to select ten people for our group from among the survivors. He refused to accept more than that, arguing that we might have enough guns for more than ten, but we didn't have enough ammunition. "A gun without bullets is worse than no gun at all," he told me.

Most certainly, I used nepotism in selecting my uncle, Shalom Hirsh; his son, Akiva; and my good friend Baranowski. I knew Baranowski from the ghetto; he was a butcher, a sausage maker by trade. He had brought along two Derechin girls: Sonia, a high school girl, and her younger sister, Rachel.

Uncle Shalom Hirsh and Leib, who had escaped to the forest with me, were assigned to care for our unit's horses. The three new women, including Sonia and Rachel, went to work in the kitchen with Kolya. Baranowski, besides working in the kitchen curing meats and making sausages, also served as a regular fighter. The other six men I had selected were assigned to the fighting unit. All six had done military service before the war, so they caught on to our weapons quickly.

More Jews escaped to the forests as other, smaller towns were liquidated. Among them was Dr. Yehiel Atlas. Although Vanya's group received the survivors well and opened their kitchen to them, the younger Jewish survivors organized their own unit. The Atlas group was named after Dr. Atlas, its original leader. Vanya's men helped these fledgling warriors with supplies and ammunition; their other needs were supplied by local farmers. For armaments, they retrieved weapons from the Shchara River and restored them to working condition.

On December 21, 1942, the Germans attacked the Partisans in great force. Atlas, leading his group from the front, was killed.

Every unit in the forest had a weapons workshop. Rifles left behind by the Russians when they retreated were recovered and reconditioned. Still more weapons were donated by local people. Some informed the Partisans about people who had hidden weapons.

The greatest problem was the women, children, and old people. Our Supreme Command ordered us to organize a family camp away from the fighting groups for the noncombatant element of the Underground. For the time being, the family camp could remain in the Boroloom Forest, in an area where the trees and brush were not as thick. In the beginning, the Underground treated the newcomers fairly, but later this changed. The three hundred escapees were suffering from hunger, disease, and lack of clothing and shelter. They were not kept informed of the Nazi patrol movements, making them vulnerable to the brutal hunters. Barely one in ten of them survived till the war ended.

Dr. Rosenzweig, a survivor from the Derechin ghetto, whom I knew well, offered his skills to the secret infirmary. Eventually this infirmary was converted into a regular hospital with four well-trained doctors on staff. The Jewish members of the Underground were instrumental in smuggling doctors out of the ghettos and bringing them safely to the forest to work for the Underground. One of these physicians, saved from the Lida ghetto by the Jewish Underground, was the legendary Dr. Miasnik, who survived the war and eventually emigrated to America.

The prewar Jewish community had lived a life of strict morals; chastity was the rule, and adultery was a sin. The war changed all that. Under the pressures of life in the ghetto and the Underground, men and women formed strong attachments and shared with each other unreservedly. Some girls couldn't adapt to this freer life, and having isolated themselves as a result, died because they had no one to help them survive. Many girls and some of the older women were anxious to get into the fighting units, where they could provide their own security and shelter and not rely on men.

For the Jews in the forest, a new way of living had begun. We had not stopped believing, but we no longer practiced our beliefs. The only way to tell us from Gentiles was that we spoke Yiddish in the family camps and in the Jewish fighting units. Social standards changed. We could not and did not marry; instead we chose our mates through mutual consent. People married without weddings, and babies were born without doctors, midwives, or hospitals.

No girl was safe from the Partisans, who were highly promiscuous. When Baranowski first came to our camp, he and Sonia, the older of the two sisters, were secretly married. To protect Rachel, Baranowski asked me to declare her as my girlfriend from Derechin. In that way, we would be justified in asking the commander to marry us officially. I wasn't comfortable with this plan—all I wanted at the time was to kill Nazis—but I told Baranowski I would willingly declare her my steady girlfriend, just to protect her from the others.

It amazed me how even in these circumstances, under the constant threat of death, life went on. Men and women became romantically attached, and in the breaks between battles, they expressed and satiated that love.

I became a favorite of my commanders, Vanya and Vasya. They taught me all they knew about warfare, armaments, and security. I was eager to listen and learn. This personal friendship enabled me to keep my uncle and his little boy in our unit. To my regret, I could not spend much time with them because I had so much to do—Vasya and Vanya relied on my efficiency.

Each time I returned to camp it pained me to see my uncle struggling to care for Akiva. I sometimes worked up the nerve to suggest to my uncle that he marry again, so that he would have help caring for his little son. He rejected this option, stating flatly that his own existence mattered little to him and that his son's future was all that kept him going. Many people had this attitude: they had escaped the Nazis, but it didn't follow that they had the will to live.

The younger people among us, the ones without prewar memories of life and family, could not comprehend how different war was from the peace their elders once knew. The constant struggle to survive, and the loss of their loved ones in the most mindlessly brutal circumstances, made them callous. Though people now looked out for themselves, the ghetto had not destroyed Jews' ties to one another. We gathered around the camp bonfire at night and reminisced, discussing our memories and tragedies. The Russians were in another group, singing, joking, and laughing. They would try to empathize with our bereavement, to remind us that they, too, were far from their homes and families, and that they didn't know whether they were safe and well. Even so, we Jews felt we had to conceal our sorrow, keep it within ourselves, and show happy faces to our friends the Russians.

We could not help but respect the Russians for their endurance and for their dedication to the struggle, to the cause of "freedom from the Nazis and a return of the Soviets." Seldom did we hear them talk of home, their families, or the friends they had left behind. Perhaps this was because the communists had taught them that family must come second to the state and to the Party.

14

SOON ENOUGH WE RECEIVED yet more Jews, escapees from the nearby ghettos of Zshetel, Novogrodek, Kozlowshchyzna, Bielica, and Dvoretz. At the time there were still ghettos in Dvoretz and Lida. The Zshetel Jews were well known to us; one of them was the heroic Alter Dvoretzki, a dynamic man, an attorney by profession. Under the most hopeless conditions in the Zshetel ghetto, he dared to organize a resistance group. He needed weapons and ammunition and got them from contacts outside the ghetto. Then he escaped to the forest, organized a resistance unit, and helped other escapees join the fight against the Nazis.

Dvoretzki knew that Samek and I had already asked our commanders to raid Derechin. Now he himself appealed to the commanders to attack Zshetel. The commanders categorically refused his request. It was rumored that they didn't trust his judgment. Dvoretzki was well liked among his men, who were deeply loyal to him.

Kolya, the commander of the Lidsker *otriad,* was suspicious of Dvoretzki and resented his arrogance and disobedience, and he began plotting an ambush against him and his assistant. Kolya and his men killed both and burned their bodies beyond recognition. The Partisan commanders tried to cover up the murder by spreading the word that Dvoretzki and his aide had been killed by mistake. Even so, the Zshetel Jews in the Underground soon found out that the Underground had eliminated him.

The Zshetel ghetto was liquidated on August 6, 1942. Some of its survivors organized a separate Jewish *otriad* consisting of two groups, one led by a Russian named Kolya Vahonin, the other by Hershel Kaplinsky. Their "patch" was on the far side of the Shchara River in the Lipitchanian Forest. These Jewish fighters, escapees from the burning ghettos, replenished our ranks and strengthened our resolve—our cause was worth dying for.

As the number of escapees from prison camps and ghettos continued to increase, a unified command was established for all units on both banks of the Shchara. The groups became better organized and integrated into brigades and battalions. Each brigade had its own staff under the command of a battalion commander. Ours was none other than Commander Boris Bullat, the one-handed fighter.

Late in 1942, new Soviet political appointments were made, and we began to feel their influence. All groups, including the ones in the Nalibokie Forest, were assigned to a single commissar. From that point on, the Underground forces in Belarus would be led by the Soviets.

Having been strengthened, the command decided to raid Derechin. We Jewish fighters knew we wouldn't save any Jews that way, for there were none left in Derechin. For us, this raid would be about vengeance. The attack was kept secret until the day came. After breakfast we were assembled and briefed about it, in the presence of all commanders. Three companies would take part in the attack: Zaicev's, Atlas's, and Bullak's. All now included Jewish fighters.

On August 10, 1942, around four in the morning, we began preparing ourselves. After a short speeches by Vanya and Vasya, we checked our weapons and ammunition. Kolka, the weapons man, handed each of us extra ammunition and two hand grenades. Our company also had a small mortar and shells. Our company would be taking along two wagons loaded with extra ammunition.

Kolka then unveiled another new weapon—a water-cooled machine gun with its own carriage and wheels called a Maxim, or as we called it, "Maximka." It was assigned to Vasya, who in turn assigned it to me and two others. We were shown how to break it down and carry it, in case we had to retreat. It broke into three pieces, one for each of us. Before leaving, we practiced breaking it down and reassembling it. Vasya was clearly satisfied with the speed with which we could do so.

At three in the afternoon, our company started toward Derechin. Only the women, Kolya the cook, my friend Leib, and Uncle Shalom and his son stayed behind at the Zaicev camp. Vanya reminded them to be vigilant and issued them the day's password.

We stopped to rest in the Boroloom Forest, where the family camp was located. The people there were mostly Derechin Jews. Vanya reassured them that we weren't abandoning them; we would be back the next day. Some of the elderly asked Vanya and Vasya to let them join the fighting. They weren't armed but they wanted to help avenge the deaths of their loved ones. Vanya agreed to take some along, but only if the High Command approved.

Our three companies joined together in the Boroloom Forest: Atlas's, Bullak's, and Zaicev's. My friends and I were gratified to see a well-outfitted Jewish company under the command of Atlas and Alek Lipshovitz, who took over after Atlas was killed. After a short meeting of the senior leaders, Bullat delivered an inspiring speech encouraging us to act like real soldiers and make this operation a success. He cautioned us not to harm civilians, who were victims of the Nazis just as we were. Then he agreed that some of the older men in the family camp could join us as volunteers.

At this, a number of the elders—old, broken-down men—ignoring the danger they would be placing themselves in, raised the sticks and branches they had armed themselves with and proclaimed: "These aren't walking sticks, they're weapons for beating our enemies to death!" Then a few more stepped forward, saying, "We're with you, comrades; let's go get even with our bare hands!"

This scene touched every fiber of the soul. Their call for vengeance urged us on and strengthened our will to root out the Nazi barbarians. It was the fulfillment of a dream. Now we Partisans, fearless to the last, marched toward Derechin, unified in our hearts and deeds against a powerful enemy, ready to die for our freedom. Soon we divided our forces into different columns, each heading for Derechin by a different path. We trekked till nightfall through the woods in the direction of Slizy Podgrobelskie. At dusk we came out onto the open road and continued toward our target.

Trudging along, loaded down with my weapons and ammunition, I remembered the parting words of my Uncle Shalom Hirsh: "Take care of yourself. It's a dangerous mission you're on. Remember, you're the last of your family, so come back alive and well." I knew what I had to do, and I had sworn my own oath to punish the Nazis for murdering my family. And perhaps some of my family were still alive and in hiding; perhaps I would be able to save them. I imagined finding my relatives' murderers and punishing them now that I had the power—a thought worth savoring. I was shaking with anger and fear, and my head was throbbing with tension.

At three o'clock in the dark, thick night, our company reached its staging area in a wheat field. The three of us manning the Maximka were positioned at the top of a hillock, hidden by brush. We were off the road not far from a canal. It was the same canal I had crossed with my three companions on our escape from the ghetto, which seemed so long ago. From our position, we could see the cemetery on the outskirts of the village. Vasya reminded us that if the battle became protracted, we would have to add water to our gun's cooling mechanism to prevent it from overheating.

Our position was a good one. To start the operation, we would be firing flares at the Gestapo headquarters. We were to hold our positions till our men could get closer to the house. Atlas's company was to attack the police station and advance toward Gestapo headquarters. A brick wall built by Jewish slave labor surrounded the building and would be difficult to pass. Our company was to cover the Partisans as they advanced, and then to fall back. One more time Vasya ticked off the key points: don't leave any weapons behind; help and gather the wounded; use the Maximka wisely.

We sat alert, tense, silent. Vasya glanced at his watch, saying "A little more time." From his pocket he pulled out a bottle of vodka. "Boys, let's have a drink. Maybe these are our last moments together. Remember, fight to the end, and never surrender." He raised the bottle: *"Za Stalina, za rodinu, do pobedy."* For Stalin, for our country, for victory.

As much as I wanted to take a swig to calm myself, Vasya's slogans were not the ones I was ready to die for. I was ready to give my life for my lost family, my sister, my brothers, my relatives, the entire ghetto. I wanted to kill to get even for the evil that had been done to us Jews, who had lived in Derechin for generations. I wanted the murderers to pay for burning and suffocating peaceful civilians who had never harmed anyone. I wanted to see them beg on their knees for mercy. I gripped my gun, took a big gulp, and a deep breath, and steeled myself for battle. I envied my friends in Atlas's company, who would be fighting the murderers of our families as a Jewish force.

From our mound, in the light of a cold moon, I looked down at the cemetery, envying the dead who had been buried as Jews, with all the ceremonies, and who—if only for a while—had been remembered by someone. Grief choked me. I was anxious for the battle to begin so that my fear and rage would have an outlet. I wanted to hear the sound of the Maximka. How many would it kill? How many Nazis would plead for mercy? On the horizon I could see the faint outlines of the houses of Derechin. A dog barked in the distance; the wind fluttered the leaves of the nearby trees. The rest was silence.

I spotted a shadow moving in the field and reported it to Vasya. He ordered us to take our positions. From a distance we watched one of our patrols stop the man. Soon after that, our scout crawled over to our position with new orders: we were to start firing at zero hour without any preliminary signal. Vasya and the scout synchronized their watches. I gripped the belt of machine-gun bullets. At zero hour, Vasya began firing; at the same time, we heard the deafening sound of gunfire accompanied by shouts of "Hurrah!!!"

At first there was no resistance. Then when one of our men ran toward the nearest houses, machine-gun fire erupted from the Gestapo headquarters. Vasya yelled for us to follow him toward the open road. We jumped up to follow him, aiming the Maximka toward the German fire. At the first house, we saw a grenade explode, spraying fire into the dark sky. Soon the house was on fire, the flames leaping. People were shouting: "Don't shoot! we surrender!" Two Black Crows and some other people ran out of the house. At the same time we heard orders from the rear: "Come out with your hands up! Throw your weapons to the side!"

Smoke from the burning house blocked our view and forced us to shift our position. In the faint moonlight we watched our first prisoners being led to the rear. The attack on Derechin was full throttle from all sides. The Germans and their police cohorts knew they were surrounded. We had thrown them into confusion. The Black Crows were the first to give up. We saw them leaving the house to our left. By then the Atlas Company had captured the police station.

After gathering more ammunition from our supply wagons, our companies advanced toward the SS and Gestapo headquarters. The Germans resisted more fiercely than the Black Crows. The three-story building with its red brick wall was a difficult target and slowed us down. The Germans had taken positions inside and were waiting for us. Having gotten this far without resistance, our boys were overconfident and stormed the building. As they approached the wall, they came under concentrated fire. Many fell. We gathered our wounded quickly and placed them on wagons to be taken to our secret infirmary.

Everything was in motion, so it was hard to tell exactly what was happening. Our couriers on horseback galloped from company to company shouting the General Staff's orders. We heard gunfire in the streets of Derechin. After a quick discussion, Vanya and Vasya ordered our Maximka to move east and join Atlas's company south of the building. Then we would storm the entrance from both sides and set fire to the building with hand grenades. Two riders arrived to tell us reinforcements were coming. Vanya told the rider to convey our new positions to them. We shouted warnings to the people in the nearby houses: "We are setting fire to you—get out or burn inside!" "Hurrah!" we roared. "Forward! Revenge! Death to the Nazis! Surrender and stay alive!"

The battle for the headquarters continued. We established our new position. Now the Atlas men assaulted the rear of the building. Though surrounded, the Nazis did not stop firing. Vasya, with a group of volunteers, including the Dembrowski brothers of Atlas's group, charged the building's entrance.

A second explosion did not budge the Germans. They kept firing their machine guns from their windows. Some of our men were calling for help. One of the Dembrowski brothers had been hit (he would later die of his wounds). Our men in the assault group set the building on fire. As flames engulfed the building, some of the Germans and their collaborators crept out to surrender. The rest of them climbed onto the roof, and the battle raged on. Blinded by the smoke, the Nazis couldn't see where to direct their fire, so they broke out through the back of their building and fled for their lives toward Zelva.

Our gun crew was assigned to yet another new position, and we aimed our Maximka in a new direction. Ambushes were laid on all roads leading to Derechin. The streets of the village were in chaos, with guns going off, riders shouting orders, fires burning, and Germans escaping.

The battle for Derechin was over. We'd won. The locals were in shock; the streets were almost deserted. We received no cooperation from the villagers. No one offered to tell us who the collaborators were. They wouldn't even complain about their Nazi oppressors.

Our commanders had arranged for wagons to be waiting nearby. They drove up, and some of us, along with a few civilians, loaded them with the weapons, ammunition, and other supplies we'd captured. These loaded wagons were then driven back to our forest camps.

Vanya dropped by our unit and congratulated Vasya on his leadership. Then he pulled out his canteen and said to Vasya and to all of us: "I salute you all for your efforts and for the victory. Derechin is ours for now."

I asked Vanya for permission to join the units searching for hidden

Nazis. He gave me a knowing look. "Okay," he said, "come along—you can show me around." Our first stop was the SS headquarters. There he picked up a brand new PPD and handed it to me.

"Keep it," he told me, "and be sure to take enough ammo for it. Turn in your rifle to the boys loading the munitions." I wanted to hug him; instead I thanked him for understanding what this machine gun meant to me. I picked up three disks filled with bullets and threw them in my backpack. I shouldered my new weapon, and we walked toward what was left of the Derechin ghetto.

The streets were deserted. Our Derechin Jewish boys were busy rounding up civilians whom they knew were collaborators. We walked cautiously, fingers on triggers. Suddenly I saw a man I knew before the Nazi invasion. My grandparents had rented rooms in his house before they were driven into the ghetto. Vanya let me stop to talk to him, after I assured him he wasn't a collaborator.

"Ivan," I said, "don't you recognize me?"

The man stared at me in disbelief: "Aren't you the grandson of the Polish refugees who were living in my house?"

"Yes, I am," I told him, my voice trembling.

He crossed himself and asked, "Yeszczo zywiosz?" (Are you still alive?).

"Yes," Vanya interrupted, "he is very much alive; he's a warrior with the Partisans."

Tears in his eyes, Ivan pointed toward the graves of our loved ones. "That is what's left of your people," he said. "Believe me, I had nothing to do with it. Would you like to come into my house?"

I told him we would return to have breakfast with him after we had completed our task. Then I asked to Vanya for permission to visit the grave of my family. Vanya consented and even came with me. My heart was pounding as I approached the crater graves in the center of the marketplace. I could not hold back my pain anymore. A scream caught in my throat, and tears streamed down my face. I cried for my brothers and sister; I wept for my grandfathers Yidl and Nuhim, for my uncles and aunts and cousins, and for all the murdered Jews of Derechin.

"Let them rest now," Vanya comforted me. "Don't cry—your vengeance will come." We turned and walked toward the ghetto. Its streets were a ghastly sight: skeletons of razed houses, vacant streets hollow with our footsteps. The smell of charred corpses hung in the air. "Grysha," Vanya said, "I see your grief, I understand your anger; I have seen enough. Let's go." Soon after that, Atlas's company arrived at the ghetto, where they, too, poured out their anguish. They hoped we would have time to build a fence around the mass grave before we left Derechin.

We were told to disperse three miles outside Derechin and get some rest. We were warned not to return to town until nightfall; we didn't want anyone to be able to count us in case the Germans returned. If any were left in the area, we wanted to put them on notice that we Partisans were a force to be reckoned with. We left a few horse patrols in the village to police the streets and relay messages as necessary.

The farmers around Derechin lamented that the Germans would target them if they returned. In contrast, the farmers nearest our camps would greet us as heroes on our return, offering us drinks and shouting slogans: "Long live the USSR!" "Long live Papa Stalin!" "Long live the fighting Partisans!"

During our breakfast at Ivan's house, we heard gunfire. We grabbed our weapons and ran outside. Our riders sped in the direction of the shots. Quickly the streets of Derechin filled with Partisans racing from different houses. At first we thought the Germans were back; however, Vanya judged that the shooting wasn't intense enough to indicate German strength. He decided the shots must be coming from our own patrols.

Vanya stopped a rider and asked him what the shooting was about. The rider told him the Atlas boys had found a Black Crow hideout. The Partisans surrounded the house to capture them alive. Soon the shooting stopped, and we saw a line of barefooted prisoners being marched toward our General Staff on the outskirts of the village.

The non-Jewish commanders discreetly let the Jews handle these prisoners. There was some satisfaction watching these sadistic policemen begging for mercy from Jews. The fire of revenge burned that day. The Jews shouted at them: "Where was your mercy when you forced the Jews to dig the pit? How many horses or pigs did you accept from the Nazis for every Jew you killed?

The men of the Underground were ready to celebrate. A party was held in Slizy Podgrobelskie. Vasya took me along as his bodyguard, directing me to take care of him when he got drunk. At my own request, I was placed on guard duty while the others celebrated. Outside, alone, I had time to think again about the battle won and the lives lost. Vengeance had not helped as much as I had hoped, or perhaps I hadn't taken enough of it yet. My Jewish brethren were still dead, and my Jewish heart still ached with inconsolable pain.

15

WHEN WE RETURNED TO CAMP, we were greeted impatiently. Kolya wanted to know how the Maximka and all the other weapons had performed. They slapped our backs and congratulated us on our victory. I was anxious to find my Uncle Shalom and let him know I was safe.

In the afternoon, our commanders and the rest of our company appeared. They were sober by then and told us Bullat would be joining us that evening. For their arrival, the camp was placed under tight guard. We were warned not to speak to or question the prisoners. Finally, a rider approached to announce the High Command was approaching.

Once they arrived, we brought out the prisoners barefoot, blindfolded, and tied to one another with ropes. Two were Gestapo officers, the other eight Black Crows. We now put them on trial. Although we called these gatherings military tribunals, we weren't too concerned with technicalities out there in the forest and did not follow strict procedures. All of us well knew just how bestial these people were.

We expected that all ten would be executed, but, to our surprise, two Black Crows were spared the executioner's bullets. All of us understood that this was a political decision. These two were from a district where support for the Underground was strong, and their family's intervention probably saved them. Also, we hoped that by saving these two, we would be encouraging the Germans to treat their Red Army POWs more humanely—at that time, Russian POWs were being murdered and mistreated at will by the Nazis. It was also considered that these two were new to the police and had been drafted, at that. So both were permitted to join the Underground, though we would be watching them closely.

The prisoners were told to strip—their uniforms were too valuable to soak with blood. Then the firing squad assembled. I was not assigned to this detail but was glad for the chance to listen to the condemned beg for mercy. It was almost soothing to hear the "master race," these "Aryan gods," ask for permission to turn their backs so they wouldn't have to look death in the face. We buried them in an unmarked common grave.

These military tribunals were the same in every camp, and very few prisoners escaped the death sentence. Vanya and Vasya did not want to have to guard the two captured men we had saved from execution. "Besides," they contended, "once a traitor, always a traitor." They turned out to be right when some of the Black Crows stayed with us just long enough to help the Nazis set up an ambush against us, with bloody results.

There were other forms of treachery. Men would present themselves as Russian POWs who had escaped, and would infiltrate the Underground. Once they knew our strength and whereabouts, they reported these back to the Germans. Because of such incidents, we began screening new recruits with far more care. This caution made it even more difficult for Jewish escapees of the remaining ghettos to join the Partisans.

Our victory at Derechin marked a new era for the Underground. Our power by then extended from Baranovich to Zelva and from Novogrodek to Grodno. More and more civilians began supporting us. The Germans had burdened the farmers in the region with heavy taxes and produce quotas and allowed them to keep only the bare minimum for their own use.

After Derechin, we controlled the town and its surroundings for over two months. We took over the two mills and let the farmers use them for free. The village also had a small slaughterhouse, and the Underground made good use of it as well. The farmers could use it, but mostly we did. Baranowski, the sausage maker, took charge of it and produced a variety of sausages and smoked meats, which he stored in barrels or cold cellars.

The farmers appreciated our generosity and began to respect us. Many now saw us not as bands of robbers but as trustworthy people dedicated to their welfare. In return, they shared their grain with us. In that way the arrangement with the mills and the abattoir served both groups.

Even the most hostile farmers began to warm to us, to trust us, to cooperate with us. They passed us valuable information, for example, telling us who the local collaborators were so that we could eliminate them before the Nazis returned.

On a hot October morning, people from the outskirts of Derechin galloped their horses into the village in a great panic: "Children of God, run for your lives! We may have to run with you. The murderers are coming back, from all directions, hundreds of them!"

An immense force was approaching the village from three sides—east, west, and south, the Slonim, Zelva, and Piaskie roads. Men, wagons, horses, and supplies were all heading our way. Our camps were to the north, and there were no invaders yet in that direction. Soon enough, we informed our command that the Germans were threatening to retake Derechin. All day, couriers traveled between the companies and the General Staff posts, keeping orders flowing. By nightfall all our companies had been shifted to new locations.

At times like these our informants, fearing retribution, would follow us into hiding till the storm blew over. They would even move their families to settlements near our forest camps. Our High Command didn't mind this—informants were valuable enough to be treated well.

The ferry over the Shchara River worked overtime that night. The family camps had been alerted to the danger and told to prepare for a fight. Many of these civilians in our care fled across the river to an even larger forest.

North of Derechin, only two companies remained south of the Shchara. Bullak's was positioned near Ostrova, Vanya's near Slizy Podgrobelskie. Our new camp was near the village of Volia. There we split into several units. At nightfall we took up a position on the edge of the forest. I was again assigned to the Maximka under Vasya's command. In the morning we moved again after Bullak fought a skirmish with the Germans. We were to cover his company's retreat into the dense forest across the river.

We retrieved a new weapon from the river—a light cannon, which one man could maneuver easily. Kolka, our weapons man, restored it for us, and we placed it in our new position.

One of our scouts found us and told us about Bullak's fight the previous day. Comrade Bullak was a simple man with no training as a military strategist. He had conducted the battle relying solely on his common sense. He had set up three defensive lines in a half circle. In the first were men perched on tall trees armed with light automatic weapons. From there, they strafed the enemy, but only from the side, to give the impression that our line was on that side. Confused, the enemy retreated to positions facing the side from which the bullets were coming. Then our second line opened fire on them from behind. Even more confused, and believing they were surrounded, the enemy retreated straight into our third line. After a few hours of intense fighting, afraid to fight us at night, the Germans retreated in disarray, firing on their own soldiers. Their losses were heavy.

The scout alerted us that a column of Panzer armored cars was heading our way along the Derechin road toward the Shchara and the village of Slizy Podgrobelskie. Most of the local people had fled to the dense forests across the river. Many had released their livestock to roam free, but some took their cows with them into the forests. We heard the cattle mooing in the forest as the refugees approached our position. Soon after, we heard the roar of the Panzers as the Germans entered Slizy Podgrobelskie.

We had positioned ourselves near a country lane; soon we heard horses galloping down it. Nervously, we released the safeties of our weapons. Those of us closest to the road ordered the rider to halt. The man dismounted and asked to see our commander—he had a message from Bullat.

Vasya and Vanya huddled to discuss the message. Our new orders were not to engage the enemy unless attacked first. We were also informed that the Germans hadn't yet entered the forest. They had stationed patrols at Slizy Podgrobelskie; the main German force was heading for Volia across the river.

Soon after the scout rode off, we heard the Germans shouting at the inhabitants of Volia. I knew that sound all too well, and my head and heart began to pound as I remembered how the Derechin Jews had been rounded up for massacre. The Germans were ordering the villagers to drive their livestock out of the settlement. The cattle were followed by a column of wagons loaded with loot. Soon after that we saw smoke rising—they had torched the village; we could see it from across the river. The Germans were yelling and driving the hysterical civilians toward an empty field near the river. Moments later we heard gunfire and the soul-piercing cries of the victims.

Vanya crawled over and told Vasya that we had better establish a defense facing the river in case the Nazis crossed over on the ferry. If they did, we would open fire, even though our orders were not to shoot first. Vasya considered for a moment and suggested that we give the executioners a taste of our light cannon, then another of the Maximka. After that we would establish a new position along the river bank. The debate settled, we were ordered to take up new positions. One group was stationed to cover our rear in case the enemy approached from Slizy Podgrobelskie.

From our new position we watched Volia burn. The red flames and thick smoke reached for the sky as if trying to pull back the fleeing clouds. The bellowing of frightened cattle added to the savagery of the scene. When we saw more villagers being herded toward the execution field, our commanders couldn't hold back any longer. His voice breaking, Vanya hollered, "Fire! Fire!" We opened up with the Maximka, the mortar, and the cannon. The Nazis scattered like rats, took up positions, and began to fire back. Smoothly we crossed the lane to new positions half a mile away, still overlooking the river. A few minutes later, we heard the roar of approaching Panzers. Lucky for us, we'd moved, for the Germans began pouring fire into our old positions. When we didn't return fire, they began probing for us with gunfire. Our orders were not to reply so as not to reveal our new location.

The Germans kept firing from across the river, obviously hoping to provoke us into showing ourselves. We didn't take the bait. Our discipline and bravery were tested to the full when we faced German armored cars on one flank and heavy German fire from across the river on the other. Hiding in the underbrush, we could hardly hold ourselves back. We prayed that our beating hearts wouldn't give us away. In the end, we avoided engaging the enemy. After darkness fell, we heard them retreating.

We sent a patrol across the river to Volia to make certain the Germans had left. At last we were able to join Bullak's company and get medical help for our wounded. Within an hour, the patrol had returned to describe the atrocity the Nazis had carried out in Volia.

Our commanders decided to cross the river that very night and join the other companies of our brigade—Komorov's and Bullat's—which were a few miles away. We marched back to our brigade, hungry, tired, and depressed, and asking ourselves: Was it right to keep fighting the Nazis if we couldn't protect civilians from reprisals?

In the morning we met up with our General Staff commanders, Bullak and Bullat, who were camped near Fedya Komorov's company. There we listened to a briefing about the events in Volia. The massacres had demonstrated to the local people that the Nazis were not only after the Jews—they were going to exterminate the Gentiles, too, once the Jews were out of the way. The people of Volia who hadn't fled to the forest had been murdered and thrown into two mass graves. The Germans had confiscated all their produce, cattle, and personal belongings and shipped it all to Derechin. The farmers were sent off to concentration camps, never to be heard from again.

A few hours after we joined the other two companies, the survivors of Bullak's company began filtering into camp. Bullak rode in on his white horse, jovial as always. We couldn't tell he was angry until he accused Vanya of poor judgment in not attacking the Germans as they retreated from Volia. Though he was directing his comments at Vanya, it was actually Bullat that he was charging with poor leadership.

According to him, Vanya could at least have set up some ambushes to punish the Nazis for the massacre. By our actions we were telling the Germans they were strong enough to drive us out of the district. He praised the men who *had* opened fire on them. He was certain that his own stand against the Nazis had saved the settlement at Ostrova (his home village), and that we should have done the same for Volia. In his view, the Germans having being repelled at Ostrova had turned their attention to Volia. Because they had met no resistance there, they had been able to destroy the village and massacre its inhabitants.

We learned about the casualties Bullak's company had suffered. Most of the dead were Derechin Jews. Bullak praised the boys who had sat camouflaged, perched in the trees, along the first line of fire. After he recognized the heroism of these brave Jews, our stock rose throughout the camp.

These casualties served as the catalyst for Bullak to dedicate an official Partisan cemetery. In his speech over the graves of our comrades, he emphasized the value of every single Partisan fighter and reminded us why we were fighting. Then he called for a moment of silence, during which we forgot our hunger and exhaustion and looked ahead to the battles still to be fought.

With the ceremonies over, Bullak turned to Fedya Komorov and said, "What do you have to eat for my tired men? I could use a drink."

Boris Bullat turned to Fedya. "It is our duty to acknowledge Comrade Bullak's tremendous efforts, the dedication of his men, and the losses they suffered. A drink and a good meal is what they need now." Then our commander ordered, "At ease," and we headed head toward the food line to wash up and eat.

16

THE FEELING AMONG THE RANK AND FILE was that our commanders would be looking for ways to avenge the Volia atrocity. We
had no choice if the civilians were ever going to trust us again, and we
needed their trust. After a day's rest, all the fighters were ordered to attend a meeting to learn the new plan for the coming days. It was Komorov who briefed us.

"Comrades of the Soviet Underground," he began, "a new directive has been issued today by the High Command of the brigade, to free
our people from Nazi oppression and fight our mutual enemy until victory is ours. Our farmers, forced to endure the Nazi yoke, must not be
harassed by our men—on the contrary, they must be treated like comrades and respected for their endurance.

"We have created a free zone in which we will no longer try to gather
supplies. In this zone we will only acquire information, weapons, and
ammunition. We will gather our food and clothing from farther away,
from the more dangerous areas closer to the Nazi strongholds. The Nazis
must become convinced that the districts we control aren't supplying
our needs.

"We cannot let the civilians think they will be punished for helping
the Underground. The massacre at Volia was a brutal act against unarmed innocents. The Nazis kill, rob, and brutalize civilians to avenge
their losses against the Red Army. Our victory is coming—it won't be
long before the Nazis are destroyed and driven from our Homeland.
We'll have our revenge. Further instructions will be given to you by your
commanders. *Za pobiedy, za rodinu, za Stalina!* We shall be the victorious!"

In the mesmerized silence that followed, we could have heard a pin
drop. All of us were convinced that the commissars were returning and
that we would very soon be deafened with indoctrination speeches. On
a more practical note, we were to tighten our security and send men in
various directions to harvest information and gauge the people's reac-
tion to the massacre in Volia.

Later, Vanya briefed us on the new program. We were to start burning bridges on the main roads and destroying rail lines by planting homemade mines. He himself would prepare the mines.

He assembled a group of army demolition men and assigned another crew to locate and collect shells left behind by the Red Army—the Germans hadn't found them all. These shells would be turned into mines and explosive devices for a variety of sabotage acts. At first, the site where the men hunted for shells was kept secret. However, so many men were working at retrieving shells that its location soon became common knowledge.

My friendship with Vasya remained strong. One day he asked me to join his crew, offering to teach me how to handle explosives. I could not accept his offer; I wanted too much to stay with the Jewish Partisans and my Uncle Shalom. Even so, I visited him quite often, which gave me the chance to see how bombs were made. There was some sort of chemical compound inside the shells; this was melted down and formed into blocks, ready for detonating capsules. There were plenty of shells but far too few of these capsules—a serious problem. So we had to innovate; we found that we could use the detonating capsules from hand grenades, or even attach a grenade to the mines. Both approaches worked.

At the time, the Germans weren't guarding the railroads carefully, so our sabotage work was quite successful. We slowed them down by blowing out bridges and destroying rail lines. Our High Command had made contacts among the railroad workers and thus obtained information about which supplies the Germans were shipping on which trains. This meant we could place explosives in critical places at the right times and destroy supplies the Germans badly needed at the front.

Most of the demolition gangs had three to five men. These crews were kept small, the better to stay hidden. At first, our mines consisted of an explosive attached to a capsule attached to a chain. The mine was placed under a rail, preferably on a rise where the rail line curved, so that the train would derail and possibly even turn over. After placing the mine, we tied the camouflaged chain to the ring of the capsule. One of us, the detonator, hid in the brush and waited for the train to approach. He then yanked the line to detonate the mine, once the train reached the middle of the curve. At the sound of the explosion, everyone ran for safety. Later, our informers would tell us how much damage we had done.

The Nazi propaganda did not disclose these incidents or the damage we were inflicting. What the public could read were accounts of executions. Example: "The Nazis killed a number of bandits for not obeying the laws of the Third Reich." Eventually everyone in the Underground was trained in explosives and demolition, and every company and region was assigned a quota of demolition work. As far as our High Command was concerned, no amount of damage we did to the Nazis would ever be enough to repay the atrocities at Volia.

Plans for a new attack were being worked out, but the target for then remained secret. Meanwhile, we "liberated" a Soviet armored car from the bottom of the Shchara River. Vasya was assigned to get it running again, which didn't take him long. By then our brigade possessed two light cannons, a number of mortars, the armored car with a fully operational medium cannon, and an antitank machine gun. What we badly needed were long-range weapons.

Komorov's men found a howitzer and got it to work again. It was assigned to their group. From all of this effort to increase our arsenal, we concluded that a big operation was being planned. We learned soon enough that our next target was going to be the garrison at Kozlow-shchyzna, which had become the bane of our existence.

Summer was ending; there was frost in the air. The long shadows made playful shapes on the crisp fallen leaves. Orange and yellow foliage still clung to some branches, fluttering in the breeze.

Our companies had grown in strength and experience, having been replenished by escaped Red Army POWs. The families of these men had paid with their lives for not disclosing their whereabouts. The Germans were cutting their own throats by demanding too much food and supplies from the local people and by shipping their sons and daughters to Germany as slaves. These mistakes on their part, and our own success as warriors and saboteurs, increased our popularity among the local people. At least in our region, we had their respect again. The locals now realized that they gained nothing by helping the Nazis, whose actions were thoroughly selfish. All of these factors were going to play a decisive role in the attack on Kozlowshchyzna.

There were only two surviving Jews from the Kozlowshchyzna ghetto. One of them, Avrum Kopelovich, "Avrum the Beard," was eager to retaliate against the Nazis and Black Crows. He was ecstatic when he was assigned our new weapon, the howitzer.

After the successful attack on Derechin, the Nazis had ordered all garrisons in the area to reinforce their defenses and prepare for attacks by Partisans.

For the raid on Kozlowshchyzna we would have to develop new tactics. We were also going to have to use all our available men and equipment. The new target was nothing like Derechin. This one was close to the main road between Slonim and Lida. Because the nights were shorter in September, we wouldn't have as much time for our raid as we would have liked. Also, the garrison at Kozlowshchyzna included not only Germans, but also Ukrainians and Lithuanians, who identified strongly with the Nazi ideology. These cohorts fought much harder than the Germans themselves, absolutely refusing to surrender.

We decided to first create a diversion by burning down a wooden bridge over the Niemen River, where a small garrison was stationed. This task, which involved planting mines and soaking the bridge in naphtha, was assigned to the Atlas group. We would cut the telephone lines and encircle the nearby village of Bielica. We would then deploy in strength at both ends of the mined bridge. The point of all this was to draw German troops to Bielica, thereby weakening the garrison at Kozlowshchyzna. Furthermore, we would set ambushes all along the road to Bielica. Our men would attack the Germans and Black Crows near the bridge, far from the main garrison at Kozlowshchyzna. If everything worked, the German troops would be far away when our attack on the town began. When they tried to retreat to help Kozlowshchyzna, our outposts would intercept them on their way back to the garrison.

I was again assigned to operate the Maximka, this time with Vanya as the gunner. Midnight, September 2, was zero hour. The explosion of the bridge over the Niemen rocked the entire vicinity from Bielica to Kozlowshchyzna. The burning bridge could be seen for miles; the light of the fire illuminated the whole area. As we hoped, this action drew the Nazis toward Bielica. Artillery thundered, and a fierce battle erupted as the Nazis tried to return to their garrison in Kozlowshchyzna. They were intercepted and pinned down by our ambushes. The Germans never had a chance to return to Kozlowshchyzna. By daybreak, almost the whole town was burning. At that point, our High Command sounded a retreat, having heard that a stronger German force was approaching from Slonim.

It was during this battle that a Ukrainian shot the legendary Avrum the Beard. Avrum had single-handedly overcome a great number of Black Crows before being shot in the back. His death was a tremendous loss to the Partisans.

With our horses killed and the Germans approaching, we had to abandon our howitzer. However, a warrior named Yerachmiel Krimolowsky saved it by dragging it into the forest, camouflaging it, and later returning to rescue it. He was awarded a medal for this act.

Because our Maximka needed water for its cooling system, we experienced problems with it when we ran out. Before it went dead, we were able to destroy the bunker of the main German garrison and to keep firing long enough to shield our retreating troops.

This battle started a new chapter of bloody fighting for our company. We had gained the revenge we wanted. We had demolished the town and its garrison. There was less loot to gather afterwards, and we lost many more men than we usually did. Even so, our success proved once again to the Nazis and the local people that we were a powerful force of determined men, willing to fight on, whatever the cost.

Vasya received a citation of honor for the bravery of his company, who held their position in difficult conditions. It was determined that the retreat our leaders ordered had been justified, because of the condition of the men. They were exhausted, unable to carry on against the larger force approaching from Slonim. Although we never captured the town of Kozlowshchyzna, the Underground remained a respected force among the locals.

17

IN THE FALL OF 1942, while still with Zaicev's company, I was sent out together with my comrades Valodya and Sasha to cut telephone lines at two points between Derechin and Slonim. We arrived at the village of Maleyeh Ozierki (small lakes) and visited some local farmers to ask if there was any danger. I had known one of these farmers before the war. When his wife saw me, she looked terrified. She crossed herself and called out to her husband: "Mietch, look who's here!"

Her husband recognized me and warned me to hide immediately—Germans and Black Crows were in the settlement. The farmer could easily have turned me over to the enemy, but he and his wife were good people who would never betray a Jew. The wife told me there were fifteen or twenty Germans in the village and that they would probably leave at nightfall. I hid in their barn with my rifle. While time dragged, I contemplated my belief in God. I had been lucky again. The question that plagued me was: why?

Mietch came to tell me it was safe to come out. I left quickly, deciding it would be wiser to return to base than to search for my comrades. On the way back, I met Valodya and Sasha and we returned together. Back at camp, we told our commanders that the Germans were in Maleyeh Ozierki. They already knew, and they knew also that the enemy had confiscated two farms and arrested several farmers for collaborating with us.

A few days later we repeated the same mission, this time with more success. Some farmers with saws and wire cutters joined us to help cut the lines. By morning the Germans had restored them, with the help of farmers who were collaborating with them. So we sabotaged the lines somewhere else.

The Lipitchanian Forest remained our brigade's stronghold for the time being. The Germans were expecting local farmers to deliver their "taxes," in the form of grain and cattle, to designated locations. On a tip from informers, our High Command set up ambushes to intercept these shipments. We returned the tithes to the farmers. However, families we suspected of collaborating with the Nazis did not get their goods back—we kept their shares for our own use or to distribute to indigent farmers.

Whenever we took supplies from farmers, we issued receipts reimbursable by the Red Army when liberation came. Our stated policy was that since we were fighting and dying for the local farmers, those farmers were obligated to supply us with food and clothing. We were in contact with the commanders in the Nalibokie Forest, who in turn were receiving instructions directly from Moscow. So indirectly, we were coordinating our actions and strategies with the central authorities.

A new commander, Captain Senitchkin, was appointed to our region. A thorough reorganization followed. Each company was assigned a political commissar, whose specific job was to indoctrinate us to Soviet ways. Also established was a Special Assignment Group, which was nothing less than a unit of the secret police (NKVD). Around that time, Pavel Bullak decided to move his group across the Shchara River. His brigade was called Pobieda (victory).

Captain Senitchkin split our brigade into three smaller units. These new brigades, called *otriads*, were assigned Russian names. Our region became the model for Underground operations, famous for its successes as far west as East Prussia and as far east as Bialystok in the Soviet-occupied zone.

We Jewish fighters were disturbed by yet another change: anti-Semitism was raising its ugly head in the Underground. The Jewish fighters were being pressured to accept transfers to an all-Jewish *otriad* commanded by an easterner, a former POW named Abramov. These transfers were a hardship; we were being told to leave behind trustworthy friends. We had no choice but to obey orders and go, adjusting as best we could. I remained in a mixed group of easterners and Byelorussians; so did Baranowski; so did his girls; so did Kulakowski. My friend Samek Borenstein, with whom I first joined the Underground, was granted permission to join the Atlas group.

The same reorganization affected Uncle Shalom and his little son. They were refused permission to stay with a fighting company and were sent to the family camp. Knowing that his son would not survive the coming winter, my uncle decided to return to a still-existing ghetto nearby. He reasoned that if they were to die, death would come easier in the ghetto. I was certain he had made the wrong decision. I wanted very much to help him, yet I couldn't change his mind, so I gave him the twenty U.S. dollars I still had in my possession, the money Uncle Moishe had given me when I left the ghetto. I had sewn it into my clothes long ago. I handed the money to him, hoping it would help him survive. I later learned that he and his son were murdered when the Germans erased the ghetto. I berated myself for giving him hope with the money I handed to him. Yet in my heart, I knew that Uncle Shalom had given up. On his death, I was the only one left from my family.

Commander Vanya Zaicev was unhappy about all these changes and got into many arguments with Commander Boris Bullat. As a result, instead of being promoted as he deserved, he was demoted and relieved of his command. Soon after that, he left our area to establish an independent group based in the Nalibokie Forest.

Our commanders learned that the Nazis, incensed that we were succeeding so well at disrupting the flow of supplies to them from local farmers, were preparing to enter our zone to take those supplies by force. The resulting battles became known as the battles of Slizy Podgrobelskie. In this new phase of fighting, the Jewish warriors displayed great heroism and brought honor to Bullak and Bullat.

Before the great battle of Slizy Podgrobelskie, I was transferred to the *otriad* of Commander Abramov under a company commander named Ivlev, another easterner. Ivlev had escaped from prison and had just recently joined the Underground. He was an amiable man, always grinning. His mustache gave him a noble countenance. I was issued a lightweight machine gun and an ammunition clip, which made me the company gunner.

The battle plan for Slizy Podgrobelskie had been finalized. Once again our brigade's objective would be the road between Derechin and Volia. My group was assigned a position on a small hill, with clumps of bush as cover. The haystacks dotting the fields would help hide us. Our demolition groups had burned three small bridges the night before, and our brigade was scattered on both sides of the road, dispersed on both sides of a creek. We were to open fire only if the Nazis succeeded in crossing the river. The Atlas group was to open fire first. When the battle began, the Lipshovitz brothers and their sister were in the forward position. It was the first time that women Partisans had taken an active part in a battle.

Around ten in the morning my dear friend Moishe Ogulnik, his PPD strapped to his shoulder, rode up on his horse to tell us that Nazis were approaching our position. Their convoy included one light tank, one armored car, a number of trucks, and troops on wagons. Apparently there were one thousand of them against three hundred of us. On hearing these odds, our commander immediately changed the plan: we were to open fire only after the armored vehicles crossed the first bridge.

Tensely we waited, listening to the roar of the German armored vehicles as they approached the first bridge. It seemed that the Germans did not realize we had burned the three bridges. Their tank approached and came to a stop. One man jumped down from the tank to guide the driver across the stream, bypassing the bridge. Their progress came to a halt when the tank sank into the mud. The armored cars and trucks followed, trying to get past both the bridge and the bogged-down tank. The lead car also got stuck. The vehicle behind it turned around, probably to return to Derechin. At that point, the Germans abandoned their vehicles.

The German heavy machine guns opened fire on both sides of the road while the men on the wagons continued forward on foot, bypassing the first bridge. We didn't respond to this fire. When the Germans crossed the second bridge, the men of the Atlas group on the left side of the road were the only ones shooting back. The Germans took up positions around their tank and armored cars on the far side of the road. When their shooting intensified, our men returned fire. The Germans who had crossed the second bridge were thus trapped.

My commander, Ivlev, told me to go out onto the road and open fire at the tank. To do this I had to advance twenty yards through deep mud, so my progress was very slow; but finally I got there and began firing in the direction of the tank. Soon after, Ivlev took over my machine gun, handing me his ten-shooter recoilless rifle and ordering me to a new position. I hated giving up the machine gun and tried to object, but Commander Bullak put me in my place, demanding that I do as I was told. Following Bullak, we walked out onto the road, where we watched the tank and the armored car burning. Bogdush, one of the Jewish fighters from the Atlas group, saw a Black Crow pulling the pin from a grenade to throw at our group. He overpowered the policeman, grabbing the hand that held the live grenade while yelling at us to take cover. Then he hurled the grenade onto the road, where it exploded harmlessly. Bogdush held onto the policeman until he received permission from Bullak to kill him.

Then I saw Resha Beshkin interrogating a wounded SS soldier whom she recognized from Derechin. He was begging for mercy. I joined her in questioning him. I searched his pockets and found a picture of a girl from Derechin. Resha told me it was rumored that this Nazi had saved the Jewish girl at the time the ghetto was being liquidated. However, when we questioned him, he admitted he had shot the girl. Of course, he then claimed he hadn't been able to save her. At this, Resha lost her composure. She began yelling hysterically, demanding to know who had killed her family. Not waiting for an answer, she smashed the Nazi's head with her carbine. In a frenzy she screamed: "That is for my Mother! For my Father! For the whole family!" She turned to me, her countenance on fire, and said, "Now, Grysha, let's find some more Nazis to avenge our innocent blood."

Resha Beshkin survived this battle. Tanya Lipshovitz, who single-handedly beat a Nazi to death with her bare hands, died heroically fighting with the Underground.

In a daze, we walked on to rejoin the others. We saw more injured SS men and knew they were doomed: we wouldn't be taking them back as prisoners. Among them we recognized some tormenters from the ghetto. Vivid images of the torture and murder of our people—helpless babies and children, mothers, the aged—floated in front of our eyes. The howling we heard then was from our own souls; it was erupting as if all our loved ones were wailing alongside us. Torrents of uncontrollable tears streamed down my cheeks. Our sense of loss only heightened the urge to avenge the martyrs.

The corpses of the Germans were shipped on wagons back to Derechin, accompanied by a note signed by Bullak: "This is Soviet Underground territory. Do not blame the farmers; they are only doing the delivery. This is our gift to satisfy your demands. Excuse us for not wrapping this gift for you."

By afternoon we had finished mopping up. Anticipating a stronger force, Bullak placed our men in new positions farther from the burned bridges. Our new orders were to ambush the approaching force. The farmers who had returned the German corpses brought back information that another column of Germans and Black Crows was heading toward us in wagons and on horseback. The first few wagons came into sight. When we opened fire they turned and fled.

We returned to our bases in a festive mood. The heroes of the battle at Slizy Podgrobelskie were awarded medals. Tanya Lipshovitz was laid to rest with a hero's funeral in the Underground cemetery. The inscription on her headstone read:

> In the large forest
> In an empty field
> In the home of our brave
> With the quiver of a leaf
> Day or night

You will be remembered
This is the grave of a Soviet Partisan
Who was brought to rest!

She received a salute from the entire *otriad*. Then, deep in sorrow, we returned to our bases.

18

EVEN THE BATTLE AT SLIZY PODGROBELSKIE and the achievements and bravery of the Jewish fighters did not soften the growing anti-Semitism. Some farmers disclosed to their Jewish friends among the Partisans which of their neighbors had participated in looting the ghetto. Those farmers were confronted, and of course denied it all. When Jewish Partisans tried to reclaim what had been taken from the ghettos, these farmers spread the libel that the Jews were out to rob them. These lies, on being brought to the gentile commanders, only fueled the anti-Semitism in the Underground. The family camps were searched, and any repossessed household goods that were discovered were taken away by the High Command. This action created so much strife that some Jewish Partisans were shot as punishment.

The commanders never addressed the desperate conditions in the Jewish family camp. The Jewish Partisans were left to see to the welfare of the family camps. The Jewish family camp also served as a jail of sorts; as punishment, Jewish Partisans would be stripped of their weapons and sent there.

Baranowski was disillusioned with the conduct of the High Command. He was also worried about the safety of his wife and her sister. He kept pressuring me to marry Rachel and set up our own shelter in the forest, away from the Underground, to wait out the war. He knew where the Underground hid their food supplies and assured me he could provide for the four of us. I reminded him of the danger we and our Jewish brethren in the family camps would be in if we deserted without having been officially discharged. I also told him I preferred to fight for freedom and not to go into hiding.

Vasya Pishchulin was now in charge of his own *otriad,* which wasn't far from ours. Having established good relations with him, I sought him out. He pulled some strings and had Kulakowski, Baranowski, his girls, and me transferred to his *otriad.* Also part of Vasya's *otriad* were our old friends Kolya, Kolka, and Misha Dubakov, and some other easterners. There was less anti-Semitism among these men, who had known me since my first days in the Underground.

Resha and I had interrogated a wounded Black Crow after one of the battles, and he had told us that a girl, Sonya Shelkovitz from Derechin, was hiding in the home of a policeman. We thought he had concocted the story in an effort to buy his life, but on checking with other Derechin survivors, we found that the rumor might be true. There was a Black Crow who had gone to school with Sonya before the war and had been in love with her, and it was possible he had hidden her. One of the Atlas boys confirmed that she had tried to contact the Underground but had been ignored. Having learned all this, I got permission from Vasya to look for the girl.

The settlement where she was supposedly hidden was only five kilometers from the Derechin garrison, so the search was going to be dangerous, but I had made up my mind to try. I knew that if our High Command found out I was using an informant for a personal reason— even to save a Jewish girl's life—my own life would be in danger. Luckily, my contact had known Sonya's family in Derechin and was willing to help me save her.

She was hiding in the village of Maleyeh Ozierki. It was arranged that after nightfall she would meet me on the outskirts of the settlement. My contact and I started out. From a distance we saw the girl walking toward us wearing peasant clothes. A pretty girl she was, with glistening black hair. It was an emotional meeting, and all of us were crying as we walked back from Maleyeh Ozierki. She told us how lucky she was to have been found by us, for she needed to leave her hiding place. The policeman's mother had been about to throw her out, fearing that her son would be exposed as a "double agent." She looked ill and was worried she had been exposed to tuberculosis. The woman who hid her had told her that some Jews had saved themselves by joining the Underground. Sonya's gratitude toward us was immense. Eventually she became Commander Vasya Pischulin's girlfriend.

I still liked Rachel, but I felt threatened by a new man in our *otriad*, a Cossack named Shutoff who had been a Red Army lieutenant and had escaped from a German prison camp. A brave man and good horseman, he soon established his worth in the Underground. He became infatuated with Rachel and threatened to kill me if I kept seeing her. As luck would have it, Kolka and Shutoff went off for an evening of drinking. Kolka got drunk and disorderly and fired his rifle, killing Shutoff. An investigation declared the death an accident. Shutoff was proclaimed a hero and given a hero's burial, and once again I was able to see Rachel without threat.

As our region grew, so did the weaponry available to us, and so did the number of battles we fought. Under Commander Senitchkin, we improved our coordination with the Nalibokie Forest groups. Under Comrade Pishchulin, we started a new training program in the use of TNT and blasting caps. Again I became an attentive student. Our mines now exploded automatically when a train passed over them, giving us more time to flee the explosion site.

After a few lessons and practice runs, I was assigned to join three other men for a demolition assignment on a railroad line near Zelva. It would be dangerous; even so, I was glad Pishchulin had chosen me, for I would be gaining respect both for myself and for my fellow Jewish warriors. With Valodya we contacted a man who worked on that railroad line, who helped us evaluate the job. We learned that the Germans controlled the station from a nearby bunker and that the ideal place to plant our mine would be a high curve near a little forest.

At midnight our contact led us to the edge of the forest and pointed out the place. I stood watch on one side of the rails, Valodya on the other. The other two, who were more experienced, began digging a pit under the rail for the mine. They worked amazingly quickly. When they were done, we retreated into the forest and waited for the sound of an oncoming train. The night was still, the waiting endless. We worried we might have to leave the mine until morning and were terrified that we might have to return to retrieve a undetonated mine.

Just as we were about to give up, the sound of a whistle reached us; a train was pulling out of Zelva station, heading east. The smell of earth and fallen leaves filled our noses as we pressed our bodies into the ground, our hands over our ears. The train approached the long curve and started to slow down. Seconds later an explosion tore through the silent countryside. The first blast was followed by others and by gunfire from the train wreckage. The train must have been guarded; it must have been transporting war materials to the front.

We waited in place to learn what the damage had been. Valodya learned from our contact man that the Nazis were searching furiously for Partisans, and he was terrified of being seen talking to us. He confirmed that the derailed train had been a military one. After the explosion the train had caught fire, and the flames had made it impossible to see the damage. The Germans had gathered civilians from all around the site and put them to work clearing the damage, beating them sadistically and accusing them of being the saboteurs. When we returned to our base, Vasya praised each of us, calling us brave men. Declaring our work a job well done, he also told us to be ready for a new assignment on another rail line.

All Jewish Partisans had a hand in sabotage missions like that one. Our success drove the Germans to strengthen their defenses. In August 1942, at Ruda Javorska, the Ukrainian and Lithuanian militias established a new garrison, a large one circled by extensive bunkers. It was near a farm settlement on the Volia Diatlovo road, which was the boundary between the Duborowshchyzna and Lipitchanian Forests. Clearly, the Nazis intended to reestablish control of the region.

Soon after, our command made contact with a platoon of Ukrainians stationed at Ruda Javorska. Some became spies for us. Others were simply tired of fighting us and had come to realize that the Nazis were the real enemy. They swore loyalty to us and offered to help us destroy the garrison at Ruda Javorska.

A huge force would be needed to take that garrison, so three brigades were assembled. Vasya Pishchulin was in charge of our armored car, and Comrade Bullak of a light tank. Fedya Komorov's group from the Borba *otriad* brought their howitzer and a second armored car. We also had mortars, machine guns, and the Maximka.

The battle for this garrison was launched on October 8, 1942, at daybreak, while the enemy was sleeping. The sound of our artillery signaled the start of the assault. All bridges on connecting roads were either burned or blown up, and so was the Shchara ferry. Once our Ukrainian helpers had sabotaged the garrison building, victory was certain. We had broken up the Nazis' newest stronghold and gained the cooperation of the Ukrainians in destroying the Nazi war machine.

However, we still didn't fully trust the Ukrainians, so when they joined us, we divided them among our three brigades.

We had won many battles, yet we still felt insecure. The war wasn't over, after all. It was time to prepare for the coming winter. Leaving tracks in the snow could be disastrous, but we couldn't simply hibernate all winter; that would have been begging the Nazis to come after us and would have cost us prestige among the locals. Each *otriad* was ordered to gather and conceal food stores in various places throughout the big forest. That way we wouldn't be leaving footprints behind while searching the countryside for supplies. Another winter problem was keeping our weapons in good order without lubricants. Yet another was that the locals were afraid the Nazis would make them carry out the road-clearing tasks that had once been assigned to the ghetto Jews, of whom there were none left.

The winter of 1942–43 was bitterly, viciously cold. The snows came in early November. The Germans assembled a great force and attacked the Lipitchanian Forest, driving us out of our shelters. Later we would recall this winter as the Big Blockade of 1942. On the first day of it, the Nazis engaged us along the banks of the Shchara, intent on flushing us out of the woods and into the open. We fought valiantly all that the night on the frozen river. We took heavy casualties, but so did they.

When daylight came, a strong new force attacked our rear and advanced into the woods. It was there that Dr. Atlas was killed while giving first aid to his injured men.

The Nazis razed the towns of Slizy Podgrobelskie, Volia, Ostrova, and Ruda Lipitchanskaia. The livestock was herded away, and anyone not fleeing into the woods was killed. Soon only the name plaques of these communities were left. On the third day, the Germans had the upper hand and reached into the forests to yank us out. They cut our defenses to pieces, yet our High Command stubbornly chose to stay and fight. From that point on, it was each company for itself.

The next night, after four days of heavy fighting, we began retreating and regrouping. We tried a night retreat and found that the enemy had laid ambushes on most of the roads. Night was suddenly no longer our friend. It was decided that we would pull back through almost impassible marshland to escape the blockade. After a few days, we reorganized and tried to break through into the Nalibokie Forest.

Somehow I survived those hellish days and nights of fighting side by side with Commander Bullat of the High Command. Our one-handed commander fought bravely. He did not depend on reports from contact men; instead he personally inspected our positions and those of the Nazis. I was assigned as his runner and front man. My life hung in the balance; surely I would be either killed by the Germans or shot by my own people for cowardice or for failing to carry out a mission.

As perilous as my situation was, I felt a sense of security having Bullat always in back of me. He carried a PPD in his one hand, a few hand grenades around his belt, and an automatic pistol at his hip. His eyes shone; his face was flushed red. In battle and whenever danger threatened, he was as quick with his gun as the devil himself. Bullat knew how to identify weapons by sound. He could tell a mortar from a cannon and identify the size of the cannon.

After my first day fighting alongside him, he patted my back and told me, "You're a brave Jew."

"Commander," I replied, "you mean a brave Partisan."

"That's what I mean, Grysha, a brave Partisan for a Jew."

Every time a Jewish fighter failed to display bravery, Bullat declared that all Jews were cowards. He did not mask these insults, and he meant them to be cruel. We Jews who had survived the battles at the river felt uneasy about these comments and sensed that a new wave of anti-Semitism was approaching.

The former Atlas boys, who were now commanded by Alek Lipshovitz, thought about separating from our leaders. My friend Samek Borenstein proposed that I join them. I tried to convince him not to separate, arguing that we could not survive on our own. Besides, we would only be encouraging anti-Jewish sentiments. In the end, I stayed with what was left of the brigade.

By the end of this bout of fighting, there were only ten men left in our Pishchulin group. Only two did I consider close friends: Misha Dubakov and Vasya Pishchulin. After the Atlas boys left, Bullat asked me with dripping sarcasm, "What happened to your Jewish Partisans, the brave Atlas boys? Are they afraid of a long overnight march with their High Command? Remember, they will be held responsible and considered deserters."

I felt that his antagonism and sarcasm were directed at me. At first I was afraid to answer, but finally I summoned the courage. "Commander Bullat, I am not Moses, and I am not leading anyone. I can't assume responsibility for the behavior of any Partisan, Jewish or non-Jewish. I'm responsible for my own actions. As you may have noticed, I have proven myself a brave and valued Partisan recognized for my dedication and performance. You must be aware of my bravery in all our brigade's campaigns. You can ask my company commander to confirm my record." Vasya Pishchulin and Pavel Bullak vouched for me and asked Bullat to stop accusing me.

Captain Senitchkin then gave us new orders. "Comrades, I know you're tired and broken from the demanding fight and the long trek through this rough terrain. The heavy snow is gone, but, unfortunately, so are our food supplies. We aren't far now from the territory that was under my command before I came to you. We'll try to link the two zones to shorten our march and regain strength. Anyone leaving our brigade without permission will be considered a deserter, and according to the laws of the Underground, he will be shot.

"Commander Pishchulin is in charge and will be reporting directly to the General Staff. Anyone sick or unable to continue must report to Commander Pishchulin. We are sending a group of scouts to contact the local Underground and will proceed when we've received the necessary information."

Within a few hours our scouts had returned, bringing back some food and information that the farming settlement they reached had been abandoned—not a living soul to be found. The villagers had been murdered and most of the houses burned down. The food they had brought back had been found in some of the houses still standing.

In the morning some of us were sent out again. Our scouts spotted some women entering a house. Our men approached the women, who refused to talk to them and implored them to leave the village. They explained that the Nazis had been taking out their wrath on civilians ever since an ambush by the Underground had killed a number of Germans. Notices had been posted everywhere stating that for every German killed fifty locals would be shot. They also said that the main German force had left, though in some villages larger garrisons were being established.

This disturbing news convinced our commanders that we would have to return to our original base. While our *otriad* rested, scouts were sent out to contact the local Underground. The only news the scouts brought back was that the Germans were in control of the area.

We made our way back to our own forest, bypassing all our usual haunts, stopping only occasionally for food. As we neared our old base, we discovered that the Germans had a new method for combatting the Underground. Each village had a *samohova* (self-defense force) charged with installing a bell large enough to be heard in the neighboring villages. In turn, these villages would ring their bells to alert the next villages, and so on. When the alarm reached a German garrison, a force was dispatched to meet the threat. Vigilante committees were appointed to ring the bells as necessary. A few of these "guards" were even given arms to keep the Partisans engaged until the Germans could come up to meet the threat.

19

IN JANUARY 1943, in the bitter cold, the remnants of our three brigades returned to the Lipitchanian Forest. Besides the Germans, a new danger threatened: vigilantes were terrorizing the local people and forbidding them any contact with the Partisans. Local people were as vital to our success as air was to our lungs. They supplied all our needs. But because of the vigilantes, it was almost impossible for our scouts to enter villages or farm settlements to gather information. And information was our lifeline—without it we could not exist.

Most ominously, these vigilantes were anonymous. They brought our operations almost to a halt, and many Partisans and their contacts lost their lives after being discovered by them. The vigilantes, loathsome anti-Semites, looters of the ghettos, collaborators with the Nazi butchers, were a threat especially to the Jewish Partisans. It thrilled them to capture or kill a Jewish Partisan.

When we returned to our territory, we found the Atlas group already established and conducting operations. Comrade Bullat considered his brigade superior to them and set up camp right alongside them.

Without convening the High Command or following official procedures, Bullat used his tribunal powers to punish fellow Partisans for breaking the rules of the Underground. Two Derechin girls, Bella Becker and Feigeh Shelubski, he indicted immediately for discarding their ammunition magazines. He sentenced them to death by firing squad. He then ordered the brigade "executioner," Benjamin Dembrowski, to carry out the sentence. Benjamin, who had grown up with the girls, asked to be excused from this duty. Bullat demanded he obey the order. In desperation, Benjamin escaped, calling for the girls to follow him. Bullat and the firing squad gave chase and shot the girls. Benjamin managed to escape and later joined the famous all-Jewish Bielski brigade in the Nalibokie Forest. He survived the war, and we would have a bittersweet reunion in Naples, Italy.

I had my own problems with Bullat's baseless, spiteful attitude toward the Jewish Partisans. On returning from our trek through the marsh near the Atlas encampment, Bullat ordered us to remain in a line. I was accustomed to less formal discipline and stepped out of line to get a cigarette from a friend. Instantly Bullat ordered his executioner to disarm me. Then he aimed his pistol at me. Shocked, I was back in line before he came over. I dropped to my knees and begged forgiveness, trying to explain that I was only getting a cigarette. He stared at me with rage and hatred in his eyes. Bitterly resentful, I surrendered my pistol and machine gun, all the while watching Bullat's hand on his pistol. Just then, Commander Pishchulin, Misha Dubakov, and a few others stepped out of line in obvious protest. They reasoned with him, reminding him of my heroism and good conduct and urging him to contain his anger. Finally, without saying a word, he lowered his gun.

Alek Lipshovitz, the Jewish commander of the Atlas group, saw all this. Well aware of all the vengeful acts committed against the Jewish Partisans, and unable to tolerate Bullat's display of anti-Semitism, he stepped forward and demanded that Bullat stop humiliating the Jewish Partisans. Bullat, knowing well that the Atlas men had been urged to arm themselves and were now a force to be reckoned with, dropped his weapon and apologized.

But that was not the end of anti-Semitism in the Partisan forest. Alek Lipshovitz was stripped of his rank by Captain Bullat and replaced by a liberal easterner POW, Shubin—a mere private—as commander of the Atlas group. Even though Shubin had been a mediocre fighter and had served the Partisans only on kitchen duty, the Jewish group treated him with respect and admiration for his daring escape from the German prison. Commander Bullat was unhappy that the Atlas people had readily accepted Shubin. Before long, an exclusively Jewish Partisan group was established under the command of Ivan Abramov. Shubin was appointed to a post on the brigade staff.

All Jewish Partisans from any group in the brigade were reassigned to Abramov's *otriad*. I appealed again to Vasya Pishchulin to let me stay under his command, this time in vain. So I reported to the Abramov company. There I met an old friend, Sol Kosov, who agreed with me that a ghetto of Jewish Partisans was being created in our zone. He persuaded me to leave the Lipitchanian Forest with him.

We walked a whole week in severe winter conditions, distraught, frozen, unsure of our destination, until we encountered Jewish Partisans from our former region, who told us a reorganization was again taking place. They added that anyone not reporting to his or her assigned company would be charged with desertion, a crime punishable by death. So we turned around and returned to Abramov's company.

While we were returning, we saw yet more proof that anti-Semitism was thriving in the Underground. We encountered four Partisans from Bullak's company, who demanded we hand over to them our boots and automatic weapons. The idea of having to make this march barefoot in the snow angered me enough that I didn't care about the consequences—I grabbed my gun and threatened to shoot them. My friend Sol made the same threat. This scared them away, but not before they fired in our direction. Suddenly a rider appeared to investigate the shot. This rider, who was from Zaicev's command, ordered the bandits to report to the staff commander and us to Abramov's group. In the end they escaped punishment, but we were assigned to the "Vzvod" platoon under Alek Lipshovitz.

Abramov's company had three units. Two mixed Byelorussians and easterners; Alek Lipshovitz's was all-Jewish. We were happy to be with old friends from Derechin, and together we began building our *ziemlanka*, an in-ground shelter for the winter. Each platoon built its own *ziemlanka* by digging an eight-foot-deep pit, covering it with flat-hewn logs for a roof, and camouflaging it with brush. Saplings served as insulation and made the *ziemlanka* invisible. A dwelling's size depended on the number of men in the unit. But it was always a long room with an aisle in the middle and an oil-drum stove at the end. The "beds" were shelflike platforms placed along either side of the room. Straw sacks served as mattresses. In many shelters, the center aisle was crossed with another aisle, thus dividing the room into two more sections with more shelf-like beds.

Our ammunition and our few belongings were kept on small shelves attached to the walls over the platforms. The walls and ceilings were covered with heavy canvas; this covering served as insulation and also helped keep out the damp. Our weapons were kept on a rack near the entrance. The stove was fueled with logs to keep the place warm and dry; light was supplied by kerosene lamps. Guards were posted at all times, one inside and one outside. After curfew, which began at nightfall, no one was allowed to enter without the password.

The kitchen was outside, in the center of camp. A bell signaled meal times. Company leaders and staff slept in separate quarters. Each platoon commander shared sleeping quarters with his platoon.

We attended political lectures, during which we were instructed on communism, and the Soviet leaders, living and dead, were exalted. We spent most of our free time listening to the mournful sounds of a harmonica or small accordion and singing Russian songs of love or war. It was amazing that in spite of the dangers threatening every minute of our existence, we were able to laugh, tell jokes like in the "good old days," and find humor in our lives. In the Jewish platoon we conversed mainly in Yiddish, especially when at home base.

The men who were married or who had steady girlfriends shared quarters with the single men and enjoyed only stolen moments of privacy. To accommodate the women, we went outside to allow them to dress.

The camp had a Russian-style steam bath—an immeasurable luxury. Each platoon took its turn with the facility.

The women did the laundry. Though we tried hard to stay clean, lice were a constant problem. Each night we hung our shirts and underwear over the fire and let the extreme heat dislodge the lice. On bitterly cold mornings, we felt almost indebted to the pests for the comfort of being wrapped in warm clothes.

Each battalion had a makeshift medical dispensary that provided first aid for the sick and injured. More severe ailments and injuries were treated at the big Underground hospital, the location of which was a closely guarded secret.

Because of the cramped living conditions, the poor hygiene and the lice and other vermin, contagious diseases flourished among us. In the winter of 1943, typhoid, measles, and *swiezba* (a highly contagious skin disease) raged in the camp. Those who were infected with *swiezba* were isolated in separate shelters, where they applied a tarlike, strong-smelling substance to treat the disease. Isolation was ineffective, however, and most of us were sick with it.

For some reason, diseases hit the Jews hardest, possibly owing to a lack of immunity. Some of the affected were sent off to the family camp. The family camp—or what was left of it after the last blockade—was greatly reduced in numbers. The people there hadn't been notified of the German attack and had no weapons to defend themselves, so they had suffered the highest losses of any group. Only a few people survived, by hiding in shelters or in well-camouflaged *ziemlankas*. After the Germans left, the few surviving members of the family camp tried to relocate to the Underground's new area of operations. Many froze while searching for it; others established independent hideouts, fearing the anti-Semitism that was beginning to manifest itself in the Underground.

Baranowski, his wife, Sonia, and her sister, Rachel, along with Kulakowski and his wife and their baby, stayed in their own hideout and many times tried to persuade me to join them. Baranowski died at the hands of vigilantes in an ambush in the spring of 1943. Kulakowski remained with the women in their shelter. Sometimes I took them provisions and clothing.

The nearby settlement of Ruda Lipitchanskaia had been destroyed in the Great Blockade, its inhabitants killed and its houses torched. Some of the survivors returned to their community and began to rebuild. They began by erecting shelters against the brutal cold. That community and others like it were off-limits to our brigade. But our people provided skilled labor to help with the rebuilding.

During this time, the Underground became more self-sufficient. The food and clothing stores, the newly built bakery, and the various workshops made it possible for us to stay in the forest, with no need to approach the settlements. Even so, the long and bitterly cold winter, the hardship, the diseases, and the vigilantes together made our struggle to survive and stay intact as a force nearly impossible. Raids and demolition work were almost at a standstill. We all waited impatiently for spring.

Besides all these problems, we faced another: German spies disguised as escaped POWs were trying to infiltrate us. The Germans knew well that we were recruiting escaped POWs, so they had established spy schools in the camps and extended special privileges to those who volunteered to attend. After an eight-week course, the Nazis dropped these men into our zones. These recruits reported to the Germans whatever they learned about our activities and hiding places.

One day two young women approached some of our men, asking to be admitted to the Underground. They explained that they wanted to avoid being drafted and shipped off to Germany. On being told about them, the General Staff instructed our men to bring them in for questioning. They were granted permission to join and placed in our battalion, where we could keep a close eye on them. Soon after, one of them asked for permission to visit her home. Permission was granted, and we provided an escort to accompany her. On the way home she escaped, running straight to Derechin. The escort reported the escape to our High Command, who had the second girl brought in for questioning. Sewn into her clothing they found a document issued by the Gestapo addressed to all German commands, stating that she was a special agent who had been infiltrated into the Underground and requesting that she be given full cooperation. We executed her by firing squad.

There were other incidents like this one. Two men, Ivan and Peter, claimed to be escapees from a POW camp and were brought to Abramov's battalion. They were accepted, though we kept them under close surveillance. Soon the newcomers began asking questions about our activities and the location of the bakery and hospital. At this point we searched them and found in their possession documents disclosing that they were special agents. They, too, were executed by firing squad.

In yet another incident, I was at the bakery when a man came running in to warn us that Germans and Ukrainians were in the forest. I grabbed my machine gun and positioned it outside the bakery. I spotted a German in the undergrowth aiming his rifle in my direction. The baker, positioned next to me, fired his rifle at him while I opened up with my machine gun. An intense battle developed during which two Partisans were wounded. We were ordered to abandon the bakery, and the wounded baker was brought to camp for treatment.

So the High Command began investigating new recruits more closely than ever and uncovering even more spies. In time the bakery was moved to a new location, more guards were placed on our workshops, and all of us learned to move around much more carefully. Only then could we resume operations. Our main activity that year was demolition work: burning bridges, cutting phone lines, and mining railroads.

Somehow we had to find a way to locate and destroy the vigilantes. As a countermeasure, we appointed "chieftains" whose task it was to inform us about German and Black Crow activities in the local settlements. In effect, they were to be our watchdogs. They were also expected to provide shelter, food, horses, and wagons to any passing Partisans. This new arrangement protected the villagers from individual Partisans, too many of whom were making excessive demands on the local people. It also protected us; we knew we wouldn't be running into unexpected troubles when passing through the settlements.

20

ONE NIGHT IN APRIL 1943, a German action began. Trucks filled with German soldiers, Black Crows, and Ukrainians invaded the settlements. They set up ambushes along all roads into the forest. Some of our units began fighting back that same evening, on various fronts and in different directions. It was clear that the Germans knew roughly where our camp was. It was also clear that they intended to force us into the open and trap us in the triangle formed by the Shchara and Niemen Rivers and their front line.

When the attack started, I was off on a railroad demolition assignment between Zelva and Slonim. I was the only Jew on our team of five. Two of the men, Valodya and his cousin, were locals from a settlement near the rail line. Their parents and families still lived there. After we had carried out our assignment—blowing up an ammunition train—we returned to the edge of the forest to learn from our informant how much damage we had done. Only then, from him, did we learn that the Germans were invading the Lipitchanian Forest. We were warned not to go there—we would be stepping right into the trap. For the next two weeks, our contact kept us informed. Every day we met at a different place. News soon reached us that our brigade had left its base for points unknown. We had no idea where to look for them.

I was with comrades I could trust, yet I was still nervous about being at the mercy of four local men and not knowing where my brigade was. I was anxious to rejoin my comrades, whether they were attacking or retreating. As long as we were together, I didn't care. Meanwhile I kept my guard up and volunteered for all the hardest chores. Most of the time I stood guard duty, so I got very little sleep. When I could no longer fight off sleep, I made sure my rifle was between my legs so I could shoot anything that approached—including the men of my demolition group if they attacked me.

For the next three weeks, we took care to avoid the local farmhouses. We finally heard that our brigade had returned from the Nalibokie Forest. That same night we trekked back to find our unit.

At one settlement we encountered around one hundred Partisans from Bullak's company, who were gathering provisions. We were surprised to find a celebration going on. Certainly it was unusual for so many of us to gather at one settlement at the same time. We were told soon enough that they were celebrating the great advances the Red Army was now making in the Byelorussian sector. We were also told that after the Germans had completed their raid on the Lipitchanian

Forest, from which our brigade had fled to the Nalibokie Forest, they had conducted a similar raid on the Nalibokie Forest. Unable to defeat the massed German forces, our brigades had had no alternative but to return to their original base in the Lipitchanian Forest.

By morning my four companions and I were back with Abramov's battalion in the new camp. The next morning, the General Staff, including Boris Bullat and Pavel Bullak, came to investigate why some Partisans had not carried out their duties fighting the enemy during the Germans' assault and our battalion's retreat. Jews were accused of specific crimes against locals such as rape and robbery, as well as discarding weapons. Some of the Jewish Partisans, whether they were guilty or not, whether the crimes had even taken place or not, would be executed for them.

The following day I was stripped of my weapons and arrested, along with my friend Misha (Moishe Chaim Ogulnik). Misha was accused of taking a horse from one of our informants while on duty as a scout. I was accused of rape. The charge was that on the night my demolition crew met up with the men of Bullak's company at the settlement, I had entered a widow's house carrying a machine gun, demanding food. I had then raped the woman.

Commander Bullat, without any investigation, declared angrily that if he had caught me that night he would have killed me without hesitation. Luckily for us, our case was brought before a tribunal instead of being left to the judgment of our local commanders, whose prejudice had long been obvious.

I was called first, and presented myself in front of our General Staff, who were the investigating body. I insisted that I was innocent, pointing out that I had not been carrying a machine gun on that particular night and that I hadn't had one at any time during the Germans' recent campaign. I declared that I was ready to face the widow and that if she identified me as her assailant, I was quite ready to face the firing squad.

Misha was called next. He explained that after riding his horse ragged while carrying messages from headquarters to Abramov's brigade, his mount was incapable of continuing. He said he had had no choice, if he was to accomplish his mission, but to take a fresh horse from somewhere. His action, he argued, had been for the good of the High Command and the Underground and not for his own benefit.

The General Staff called a recess and sent us back to the stockade. Both of us were horribly worried that if the Germans attacked again, we would be shot. We were certain we had only been accused because we were Jews. We asked our friends to smuggle some weapons in to us so that we could escape and save our lives, but no one wanted to risk his life for us. We felt desperate and abandoned.

After deliberating for three days, the tribunal declared both of us not guilty and set us free to return to our company. Of course we were happy with the verdict; but we were also disappointed with our friends, and we knew our reputations had been tarnished simply because we had been charged. The stress of being accused had brought me to the verge of collapse. So we began looking for a way to leave our brigade.

The days under arrest had profoundly unsettled me. During that time I dreamed about my mother and heard her telling me to be brave and promising me she would be watching over me, that I would be found innocent of the charges. She also told me I would be wounded in battle but would recover. After I returned to the company I told my friends about those dreams. I believed that drastic things were about to happen to me.

That morning our battalion gathered, and Abramov told us our next assignment. We would be setting up an ambush on the road between Slonim and Derechin. A valuable shipment was being transported to the Derechin garrison, and our task was to intercept it. A second ambush was to be set up farther down from the first, to support the first in case the fighting grew intense.

We equipped ourselves and waited to be told the password. While we were preparing to leave camp, Alek came up to me. "Grysha," he said, "don't pay any attention to your dreams. Be brave, don't fear—we'll be watching over you. Just do your duty as a soldier. You mustn't pay any attention to dreams."

I promised to abide but asked one favor. Could I get my machine gun back? Alek searched deep in my eyes as if studying my trembling soul and told me to get a machine gun. He paired me up with Israel Kviat, who would stay close to me throughout the night.

The zone of operation was a small forest with hills all around. Our company was split into two units. One was positioned some distance away from us across the road. Among us we had two machine guns and a few automatic weapons. Most of us also had hand grenades. As usual for these ambushes, we would let the enemy pass us and then attack when they were just across the road, to create the impression that we were firing from one side only. Then the other unit would attack from the rear, to sow confusion among the enemy and prevent them from directing their fire at a specific target.

The transport column was not due until morning, but we took up positions much earlier, with instructions to hold our places. All night I was in turmoil; the dream I'd had was still on my mind. We stayed in position throughout the next day until dusk descended. Just as we were about to relax our vigilance, we heard the rumble of approaching wagons. Three Black Crows on bicycles were leading the column of wagons, which were spaced apart. We saw a few Germans among the armed men on the wagons. Alek signaled us to be ready to open fire. We let the three cyclists and the first three wagons pass, and then let loose.

The Germans began firing back. We returned fire with the Maximka and the machine guns. Shouting "Hurrah!" Alek pulled the pin on another grenade, jumped onto the road, and hurled it. The explosion was our group's signal to open fire. The Black Crows fought back hard but could not overcome us. Within a few hours the enemy was defeated, with twenty men dead and two captured alive.

In the commotion of battle while changing positions, I had tripped and fallen. Excruciating pain shot up my leg, which began swelling. Alek saw I was injured and cut my boot open and loaded me onto the wagon with the two prisoners. As the pain consumed me and my stomach turned into knots, I remembered my dream.

I squeezed the pistol in my hand and told myself I would not be captured alive. Alek reassured me he would get me safely back to camp. On the way back to Volia, I was given first aid in one of the farmhouses.

Dawn was breaking when we met up with Commander Bullak riding his horse. "Greetings to the brave!" he shouted, praising our platoon for its successful operation. Abramov was upset when he learned that the prisoners had been handed over to Bullak's custody. Even so, he commended us for a job well done.

My leg was throbbing with pain. It was suggested that I be taken to the secret hospital, but I would have had to give up my weapon. On learning that we were scheduled for action again, I begged Alek to let me stay with the platoon.

Ukrainians from Ruda Javorska were attacking our outposts. While one of our companies battled with them during the day, our battalion retreated to a new position. Last in line, I marched along clutching my pistol and hand grenade. Throughout the night we marched through thick woods, the column moving ever faster, my aching leg leaving me farther and farther behind. Hopping on one leg, I struggled to continue. I stumbled and fell again. Miraculously, I felt my joint snapping back into place, the pain subsiding. Thrilled, I called out to Alek: "I'm well again! I can walk! Please let me have my weapon back." Alek gave it back gladly. Once again I was carrying a ten-shooter rifle.

After several days we began preparing another action. Abramov briefed Alek about a new directive issued by General Ponomarenko to the General Staff of the Byelorussian zone. Every brigade and every battalion was to be assigned a quota of demolition work. Each platoon in our battalion was to destroy one train. Our platoon was to break the rail line near Volkovysk, quite a distance from our camp. In his briefing, Abramov explained that the Germans were more alert than before to Partisan activities and were building bunkers and planting mines along the treelines near rail lines. This meant each demolition assignment would now require an entire platoon.

Volkovysk had been chosen as our target because the Underground had not yet done much in that area, so the rail lines were likely to be less closely watched. The greater danger in this operation was that the target was on Polish territory, where the locals were anti-Soviet and anti-Soviet Underground. Also, we would have to cover a greater distance to reach our target. All of this was worrying us as we left our camp, with Abramov waving good-bye.

After consulting the map, Alek asked if any of us was familiar with the district. Munie Kovalski had grown up on a farm there and knew all the back roads well. Past the city of Derechin, he guided us to a settlement, where we picked up food supplies for the next day. Our plan was to cross the railroad lines near Zelva. Through people he knew, Munie found the safest place to cross the line. We had to cross on foot, but we were able to leave our horses and wagons with Munie's friends. Late that night, with the full moon low in the sky, we crossed the line near Zelva and continued on, marching in single file.

In a small forest some distance from the road, we took over a house, where we stayed until nightfall. The farmer and his wife and son were astonished—they had not encountered Partisans before. Some of the visitors in the house, whom we could not release until after we left, offered us useful information about the local Germans. One of them told us that Black Crows were in the vicinity, conscripting men to clear trees along the rail lines. We warned the farmer not to disclose our presence to the Germans, threatening him that our comrades would burn their house down if he did.

After a trek of a few hours in the dark of night we stopped at another farmstead, looking for directions for crossing the river. Munie, dressed in peasant clothes and speaking the local dialect, found out where we could find someone to guide us across. It was a farmer and his son. We couldn't be sure these people would not mislead or betray us, so we threatened to take their family members hostage.

We reached the river, where Alek sent a small group across equipped with a machine gun and automatic weapons. Once the group had positioned those weapons, Alek ordered the farmer and his son to operate both their rowboats so as to speed up the crossing. The farmer swore he wouldn't tell anyone; he said his family hated the Germans, too, and that he was amazed to see the Underground for the first time.

Our next contact, a local farmer, led us to a place where the rails curved and where our explosives would do the most damage. Three of us dug the hole, then two others placed the explosive—a mine equipped with a remote switch, which the passing locomotive would trigger. The night was dark and foreboding; the wait stretched our nerves to the limit. Hearts pounding, ears cocked, we finally heard the huff of an oncoming train and the wail of a train whistle. Then all at once the explosion rocked the ground under our feet. Right after that, we could hear the tumbling and rolling of the cars.

We quickly gathered our equipment. While we were leaving, we watched the sky light up with a red fireball accompanied by more explosions. As we fled the scene we heard Alek comment, "Looks like some gasoline tankers are on fire." The man who had led us praised our work, even saying he was proud to have helped. Alek promised him he would report his cooperation to the High Command in Moscow.

We reached the farmer's homestead and rested. The pressing matter at that point was to learn how much damage our mine had done. After nightfall, our guide went to visit a friend who worked on the railroad. Meanwhile, our platoon went back to the scene of the explosion. From a distance we could see what our guide later confirmed: the explosion had demolished a freight train with gasoline tankers and other supplies of the German army. More than half the train had derailed, and the line itself would be out of commission for many days.

We felt a great urge to celebrate, but time did not allow such frivolity. Immediately we began the trek back to base. We reclaimed our horses and wagons from Munie's friends, and only then did we celebrate. Alek went to the houses of some unfriendly farmers, German collaborators, and confiscated provisions to help us celebrate. We even found a Ukrainian collaborator, the principal of the school, and, after a shootout, captured him to take back for interrogation. After a full night and morning of travel, we reached our camp at noon.

Abramov greeted us as heroes and presented medals to Alek and our platoon in the presence of the entire battalion. The same evening, members of the General Staff came to our camp to interrogate the prisoner. He was found guilty of treason, spying, and reporting local people to the Gestapo. He was shot. The General Staff praised us for our courage. After a short break, we began preparing for a new assignment: Operation Lanceviche.

21

OUR POLITICAL COMMISSAR briefed us on the importance of our assignment—the breaking up of the vigilante stronghold at Lanceviche.

Also fighting the vigilantes was a man operating on his own, who refused to join us or to coordinate his activities with ours, a Ukrainian easterner named Maxim the Terrible. To infiltrate German garrisons, Maxim and some of his men sometimes wore German uniforms. The Germans never attributed his actions to the Underground, blaming them instead on rebellious German troops. Maxim was a legend in the Lipitchanian Underground. In one story, he dressed as a German colonel and ordered ammunition to be delivered to his post; in another, he kidnapped some high-ranking German officers and held them hostage. Both the Germans and the vigilantes told stories about his acts of revenge, which were as savage as those of the Nazis. Sometimes he left his victims hanging at a crossroads with their heads cut off.

Our leaders were critical of Maxim's methods and unhappy that he refused to join our brigade. Even Captain Senitchkin could not convince Maxim to come under his command. When in the spring of 1943 Maxim, having suffered some casualties, proposed joining forces with us, our High Command turned him down, fearing he would outshine the "regular" Underground.

The village of Lanceviche was fifteen kilometers or so south of Derechin. Most of its houses were of wood with roofs of straw or shingles, easy to set afire. In actions against the vigilantes, we had begun following a new strategy, with men from different platoons working together. I was assigned to fight alongside a man named Alyosha. Mortar fire from our positions struck the houses, setting them on fire. Victorious, loaded down with booty, we left the area in broad daylight. My souvenir from the battle was an injured middle finger.

The destruction of Lanceviche marked the first time we had carried out our own reprisals on civilians, and it did achieve our goal, which was to break resistance to the Underground. For a long time, the vigilantes did not bother us again.

Captain Kovalyov and Captain Davidov came to us from the Nalibokie Forest, signaling a new era for the Underground in the Lipitchanian Forest. Soon, parachutes were dropping men to us who had been trained for Underground warfare at a school near Moscow. They quickly began reorganizing the Underground in our zone. These Muscovites wore *pogony* (epaulets) with rank markings. Until their arrival, we had all worn civilian clothes—whatever we could gather in our raids on farms. On rare occasions one saw a Partisan wearing a Soviet cap, shirt, jacket, or insignia.

Feeding all these new arrivals became a big problem; we had to travel farther and farther afield to acquire provisions and horses.

The men who arrived with Kovalyov made changes to our equipment and methods. Our PPDs were replaced by PPSHAs. The newcomers brought with them a short-wave radio, with which they kept in constant contact with the General Staff for Byelorussia and with the Supreme Command in Moscow. They also set up a printing press that produced flyers and weekly newspapers for the Underground. The commissars were therefore better able to indoctrinate new cadets.

We built an airstrip for bringing troops and ammunition into the Lipitchanian Forest. The strip was fortified by foxholes and carefully guarded, and it was off limits to everyone. We often caught spies who were trying to gather information on the layout and defenses of this strip.

In general terms, Davidov's mission was to bring the local Underground under Soviet command. The Soviet NKVD—the secret police—was now a presence among us, operating under the name "Special Group." The Jewish survivors in the Lipitchanian Forest Underground hoped the new leaders would put an end to the existing anti-Semitism. Instead they became infected with the same scourge.

The front lines were still far from us. Even so, the Germans had a hard time stopping us from operating. Men and materials continued coming to us by parachute while the Soviet air force bombed German strongholds. The local people realized for the first time that the Soviets and the Red Army were about to return.

The Underground had grown stronger in manpower, equipment, and leadership, but the war was far from over—in some ways the dangers were greater than before. The airstrip and the flares were themselves threats. The Germans began bombing the forests, and our radio operators sometimes had to signal Moscow headquarters to cancel their airdrops. The planes would then return to base or, if time permitted, reroute themselves to the Nalibokie Forest.

Sometimes our radio men were unable to signal Moscow to stop the flights. When that happened, the pilots would drop their loads in uncharted areas. We then had to rush to recover the dropped men and supplies from as far away as the Nalibokie Forest. Many times the Germans beat us to the punch and forced the paratroops to abandon their equipment and run for their lives.

Around this time, a high-ranking officer, Major-General Kostenko, nicknamed Kapustin (cabbage), joined us in the forests. The final days of the Partisan war would be fought under his command.

The main goal of all the new arrivals was to enlist men who were familiar with Poland, especially along the border with Prussia, or who knew people in the vicinity who could be developed as informants.

On the other side of the river the people were mainly of Polish descent, and they were becoming more and more of a menace to us. The Poles were fighting the Soviet Underground as well as the Nazi occupiers. They called themselves the Polish Freedom Fighters, but to us they were the White Poles, ruthless anti-Semites. Their doctrine called for a Poland free of both the Soviets and the Nazis, yet their slogans also included, for example, "Polska bez Zydov" (Poland without Jews). It was always dangerous to venture into their territory, especially for Jewish Partisans. Most of the time they killed whomever they captured.

The White Poles controlled the banks of the Niemen River from Bielica to Grodno. The new brigades worked hard to establish themselves in that area but encountered strong resistance. Our brigades dug foxholes along the banks to establish a stronghold. Even so, our men often encountered enemy fire while trying to cross the river.

Our commanders planned an offensive against the White Poles, to be carried out by Kapustin's brigade. Several of my friends, Derechin Jews, volunteered to go along, and so did Yerachmiel Krimolowsky and I. I sensed that the anti-Semitism in my battalion was increasing, mainly because of my outspokenness, and I wanted to get away from my former commanders Bullat and Bullak. The way I saw it, the Muscovites' anti-Semitism was the lesser of two evils. I was pleased to be placed in Niewski's brigade and assigned to Suvorov's *otriad*. Because I was fluent in Polish, I was made a platoon commander. Krimolowsky was placed in charge of provisions and the kitchen.

I admired the paratroopers who had been dropped behind enemy lines, and I was inspired by watching them take on dangerous tasks. While with Suvorov's battalion, I met Jews from different regions, and I became close friends with Moishe Kaganovitz and Yankel Polachek. When I was appointed platoon commander, Kaganovitz became my aide. He was an educated man and a writer, an invaluable asset. Sometimes, for short periods, he was reassigned to Davidov's company to help publish the weekly Underground magazine.

Kapustin's brigade was to establish itself in the forest near Grodno. There were various Underground groups in the area, and our task was to consolidate them under our leadership. I was among those assigned to this work. Our group included four Muscovites, two Jews (Polachek and me), and four local men, among them Sergey Bialy. Bialy had been an officer in the Polish army and was friendly to Jews.

We would be impersonating White Poles, and to that end we were outfitted in Polish Army uniforms. We carried automatic weapons, hand grenades, and a light machine gun. In addition, we carried equipment for blowing up bridges and trains and cutting telephone lines. We were to refrain from speaking Russian. Once we contacted the Polish Underground, we were to pretend to be from the Warsaw district. To Poles we encountered, we would explain that we were on a top-secret mission involving the Vanda Wasilevska freedom fighters. Any one of us who became separated from the group was to return to a designated point near Grodno.

Our patrol along the Niemen would carry us across the river in a small boat, in absolute secrecy. Even this patrol would not know we weren't White Poles. To look like Poles as much as possible, we would travel on horseback. Once across the river, we would have to travel a great distance to reach to our destination.

The crossing took place at night under the watchful eye of our comrades. Around two in the morning we stopped at a farm settlement to gather information for our advance. Sergey and two local men entered the farmhouse. The rest of us guarded the horses and patrolled the outside. As usual, the barking dogs were an irritating menace. The farmer who came out to investigate the commotion eventually invited our men inside. Not suspecting that we weren't White Poles, he fed us, and we took turns going inside to eat.

The farmer mentioned to Sergey that there were some Soviet Partisans near Mosty, our destination. According to him, they were bandits who raided the local people for food and supplies. From his comments and tone of voice, we knew he was collaborating with the White Polish Underground.

Sergey, pretending to be sharing a secret with him, told him we were Polish Underground fighters from the Warsaw area and that we were seeking to contact our fighters in this zone. He warned us to be on the lookout for the Soviet Underground while we were searching for the Polish Underground around Mosty. Glad to help, he suggested that we stay in his house for the day and start out the following night. He told us he had a brother living at a small farming village near Mosty who would cooperate with us. We accepted the farmer's hospitality. We even let him hide our horses in his stable.

Our commander asked Sergey to tell the farmer we would be taking along his son as a guide to his brother's house. The farmer was apprehensive but agreed after we reminded him of the importance of our secret mission.

We saddled our horses and were off. The ten of us followed the farmer's son, who seemed to know all the shortcuts. It was a hard ride for us and our mounts. The rain fell all the way. Our column was spread out so far that only the sound of horses' hooves enabled us to follow the man ahead.

It was nearly morning when we arrived at our destination. The farm was on a hill surrounded by a small forest—a favorable place for a stay. Following military procedure, two of us stood guard while Sergey sent the boy to get his uncle. This man was a typical Polish farmer with a waxed mustache and puffing on a large, curved pipe. He bowed to Sergey and greeted us in a country dialect: "Good morning, honorable soldiers. I have the pleasure to welcome esteemed guests. Long live Poland and all the honorable knights who wish to bring our homeland back to the people. My house is yours—welcome."

Sergey, in an obsequious manner, promised that he and his brother would some day be rewarded for helping the Polish Resistance. He hoped we would not be a burden while staying with him. After a hearty meal and some drinks, I tried to stay away from the conversation, which, of course, involved slandering the Soviet Union and the Jews.

Soon the farmer began telling jokes in which the Jews were the main theme. I kept my feelings in check and joined in the laughter, but inside I was on fire. Glancing in my direction, the farmer suddenly had a revelation and said, "My honored soldiers, one of you here looks like a Jew. I hope I'm mistaken." Sergey burst out laughing and with bravado told the farmer he'd had too much to drink if he couldn't tell the difference between a Jew and a Georgian (me) who had deserted the Soviet oppressors and was now fighting to restore Poland to the Poles. More toasts followed, and the farmer apologized to me. "Forgive me, honorable soldier, for my ignorance. What would a Jew be doing among such brave men anyway?" For the farmer this was a joke; for my comrades it was a close call; for me it was a realization that Polachek and I were a liability to our group in the White Poles' territory. I wondered what choices my comrades might make if their lives were endangered by our presence.

Polachek was also troubled; he worried that our comrades might murder us; the anti-Semitic poison could be found in even the least suspected hearts. We vowed that we would look out for each other and never let our guard down. If we were truly threatened, we would go down fighting for our lives and our honor.

Evening and its darkness pushed us on our way again. Sergey and the farmer led the way, riding side by side. The rest of us followed single file, spaced apart. I made sure to ride last. Eventually we reached a farmhouse near the small town of Sabakincy. A new informant told us a group of White Pole Underground men had just been there and that he could direct us to them. Sergey, thinking fast, told him we ourselves would first have to contact the people we needed to see. This farm was also a good place to spend the day, sheltered as it was by a forest. When we asked the farmer for directions to Swiente Blota (Holly Mud), he told us we needed to be careful because that was Soviet Underground territory—most welcome news to us, even though we could hardly tell him so.

This farmer introduced us to yet another cooperative farmer, telling him we were searching for a man named Paul. Appalled, the farmer told us, "The man you describe is a Byelorussian!" Once again Sergey explained that our mission was top secret. The farmer was convinced and offered to lead us to the man we had described.

Sergey told the farmer we needed two suits of civilian clothing. The farmer gave us directions to a farming tailor in the area. However, he did not want the tailor to know he had disclosed the shop's location to us. Sergey promised we would speak Russian and act as if we were Soviet Partisans out to rob him, for we would not want to disgrace the Polish Army's good name.

At the tailor's, three of the Muscovites had themselves outfitted in civilian clothing but kept their Polish uniforms for the time being. The farmer then left us, happy to be of service to his countrymen the White Poles, and we continued on our way. Riding through the forest without a guide, we felt more at ease, with just our own Soviet Underground company.

22

WE FINALLY ESTABLISHED CONTACT with the Soviet Underground. On a drizzly autumn evening, taking the usual precautions (passwords and so on), our commander found our three contacts, who offered to lead us to their camp. We could not keep our horses, so we asked our guide to hide the saddles for us and let the animals run free. Trudging through the wilderness on foot in cold, rainy weather proved quite strenuous.

There were only about twenty-five of these Partisans. They slept in portable army tents. They were poorly equipped, possessing just a few automatic weapons, and they were astonished to see how much better equipped we were. Our effort to come all this way to help organize a properly functioning Soviet Underground was celebrated with toasts.

The Partisans there were just beginning to organize themselves. Most of them were draft dodgers, POWs, Red Army deserters, and escapees from German labor battalions. No organized sabotage work was being done. Because they posed little threat, the Nazis were not afraid to enter the forests. Our new comrades complained that the Nazis were protecting vigilantes and tolerating White Poles but ruthlessly pursuing them. Because this camp was surrounded by hostile locals, its discipline had to be far more strict. There was no shouting and the fires were kept small. They were always ready to shoot.

That first night, I learned there were two Jews among these men, the only survivors from the ghetto in a nearby small town. We were delighted to find each other. They were sad to be the only survivors and afraid of being hunted down as Jews. Out of natural caution, we tried not to stick together, but secretly I was glad to be sharing a tent with one of them. From him I learned that some Jews were hiding in nearby family camps. On learning that many Jews were fighting in the Underground farther east, my tentmate told me he would volunteer to guide us when we returned to the Lipitchanian Forest. His intention was to remain with us. The Jewish boys assured me that their commander would not object to them leaving. Besides, as our guides, they could provide us with a great deal of intelligence.

There was demolition to be done in three places. Each group was assigned a local guide. My group was assigned to cut telephone lines and blow up a small bridge on the road from Lida to Grodno. The second group, with Polachek, was to burn the property of a wealthy farmer who was collaborating with the Germans and had brought about the deaths of many Soviet Partisans in the zone. The third group, the smallest, was to cut the phone lines along two roads leading to our operations. Each group was also to "bomb" the farm of a local collaborator—that is, raid his house for clothing and other supplies for the entire group.

We were told that the vigilantes and White Poles were active in the farming villages but not on isolated farms. Ours being a small Underground group, we didn't have enough men to guard the camp while we were carrying out our raids. So we had to dismantle the camp and hide or camouflage everything to make it look as if we'd left the area.

I was with Sergey, Valodya, the two local Jewish fighters, and a few other local men. It was an exhausting, dangerous trek through forest, marshes, and muddy fields. When carrying out "bombings," we impersonated Polish Underground fighters, the point being to discredit the White Poles with the farmers. From the farms, besides food and clothing, we took naphtha, saws, and axes—the farmers would miss these things most of all. Of course we had to carry them with us along with the supplies we'd brought from base camp.

Our objective was a bridge. The road it was on, like most Polish roads, was paved with small cobblestones. All was quiet, no traffic to be heard. We divided ourselves into three units. One was placed to guard both ends of the bridge; another went to cut down the telephone poles; the third was to place the explosives under the bridge. We splashed naphtha all over the bridge. After the mine was planted, we set small fires at both ends. The patrol at the other end of the bridge crossed back and then placed themselves as backup guards for the rest of us. The telephone poles were down by this time, though the wires themselves would not be cut until the bridge was in flames. We exploded the mine using a long fuse, which we lit with a cigarette end. This gave us time to escape before the detonation. From a safe distance in the forest we listened to the explosion, which sent burning chunks of the bridge flying. Smoke veiled the entire area, and the fire's intense heat drove us deeper into the forest.

In our "bombings" we had picked up enough *samagonka* (moonshine) to celebrate our success. The merrymaking was short but intense—plenty of booze, cold sausage, ham, and good black bread. The precaution of not building a fire was enforced. Fearing retaliation for the demolition work, we relocated our camp a good distance away.

We still needed to establish contact with other Underground groups in the area. Our Muscovite commander ordered the local leader to get word to another group that we would be stopping at their camp. Three local Partisans were sent as scouts to contact the other company and summon their commander to meet us. Two days later, the men returned with the commander and his aides in tow. The men were astonished to learn about our sabotage work. The Germans, they told us, had not blamed the Soviet Underground for the sabotage; they thought it had been bandits hiding in the forests. The locals who had been conscripted to repair the bridge brought back the news that the phone lines had been destroyed—also our work. The local people did not see our activities as revenge against the oppressors. Rather, they were angry with us for creating work without pay for them.

From this other commander we heard the rumor that Soviet Underground men, claiming to be paratroopers and Muscovites, were roaming the area. Were these people German spies? The commanders decided to investigate.

The following night we hiked toward the place where the suspect wanderers had been sighted. Soon enough, not far from our camp, we encountered them. Actually, they were men from our brigade on an assignment, and they weren't disguising themselves as White Poles. They gave us some useful advice for our return journey. With them were several women, wives of Red Army soldiers who had avoided registering for work in Germany. Instead they had joined the Underground. We were thrilled to find four Jewish men among this group. We stayed in the area for two more days before starting back to the Lipitchanian Forest.

On our return trek, we were to sabotage a train near Mosty. This time we took forest paths with local guides. It meant we could wear our own clothing, which we much preferred, instead of Polish uniforms. Even wrapped in long Red Army overcoats, we suffered badly from the bone-chilling cold. After two nights of walking and two days hiding in the bush, we reached our assigned target.

We busied ourselves placing the explosives near a rail crossing not far from the main road. Lucky for us, the Germans did not watch this spot. The detonating capsule had a ring attached to it and a piece of gun-cleaning rod within the ring. Whichever side of the ring the metal rod was pushed to, the detonating capsule's hammer would strike the firing pin and set off the explosion.

Sergey placed the rod in the ring, and I placed the mine in the hole. Just as we were leaving, my overcoat accidentally brushed the metal rod. I froze on the spot, my feet glued to the ground, and raised my eyes to heaven. I told myself, "I'm about to be blown to smithereens." The metal rod quivered but did not touch the ring. I heard Sergey calling, and his voice brought me back to reality and sent me running for safety like the rest of the men. My tongue was too dry for me to reply to Sergey's scolding.

Shaking like a leaf, I asked my commander for a drink. The vodka released the tension and made me laugh like an idiot while we waited for the explosion. After more than an hour, we heard the wail of an approaching train, and my head cleared instantly. Rolling along at full speed, the train tripped the rod. An explosion rocked the area and reverberated through the forest. The sky turned red, blazing with fire, and the earth shook. Smoke filled the air, and from afar we heard the screams of the injured. Running as fast as we could, we distanced ourselves from the explosion.

By dawn we were near the Niemen River and looking for a ford. We accosted a group of fisherman and demanded they row us across. They turned out to be White Poles from nearby farms. We encountered some Germans, who opened fire on us. We did not fire back, changing direction instead to evade them. During this episode, a hand grenade hit a barn and set a haystack on fire. The thick smoke and intense heat slowed down our pursuers, and we were able to vanish into the forest.

In the chaos, we all ran in different directions. As a standing order, we were to regroup at Piaskie, a village near Derechin. With the fire lapping at my heels, I reached the forest's edge. Beyond lay an open meadow. I had to make a quick decision. There was fire behind me and open ground in front of me where the Germans could pick me off easily. With no time to waste, I just kept running till I dropped. While I was catching my breath I heard footsteps. It was Valodya, who was as lost as I was. Crouching behind some bushes, we watched the night sky turn flaming red, reflecting the burning farm.

Bones aching, eyes red from the smoke, exhausted, we kept walking. When we couldn't find the others from our group, we stopped to find shelter for the day. The following night, we went searching for our comrades. After wandering for hours, we found ourselves back at the Niemen. After walking for hours along its bank, following the stars, our stomachs growling with hunger, we found shelter for another day.

The following night, after wandering for a long time, we concluded that we were going in circles and would have to ask someone for directions. At one of the farmhouses, we were told that we weren't, in fact, far from our base. We confiscated two horses from the farmer and headed to Valodya's farm to rest and regain our strength.

Before going on, we wanted to learn what had happened in our zone while we were gone—a precaution we always considered important. Valodya's mother welcomed us and insisted we hide with her for a few days to recover our strength. Our horses needed rest and grazing and received the same welcome. After a week's separation from our group, we finally rode into camp.

It was good to be back with our friends. My Jewish friends were my family now, and their elation gave me a sense of belonging. We were glad to learn that all of us had returned safely.

There were no fanfares, rests, or vacations. Life as a Partisan was a constant battle to throw off the yolk of occupation, to resist the enemy, to liberate ourselves and the local people.

The next battle turned out to be the biggest we fought in. We were heading back north to Grodno, an area controlled by the White Poles. These people, Polish freedom fighters who called themselves the Armia Krajova, were fierce anti-Semites whose motto was "Kill the Jews, then the Germans." We were constantly on guard against them.

This next mission was filled with danger, fire, and battle. We headed back to the Niemen for the crossing. In the action from which we had just returned, we had been only a small group of scouts disguised as White Poles. This time we started out in broad daylight, with no disguises, three thousand of us armed with light cannons and heavy mortars. Radio personnel had been assigned to each brigade to maintain contact with Byelorussian Underground headquarters as well as Moscow. Just like a regular army, we crossed the Niemen and continued north toward the forests around Grodno.

We marched for two days and two nights, destroying bridges and cutting phone lines. Pushing forward, we overcame the White Poles' resistance. On the third day, a strong German force attacked us—two infantry divisions supported by planes, tanks, and heavy artillery. They dropped incendiary bombs that turned the surrounding forest into an inferno. Outmaneuvered, we fought bravely for three days and three nights. Finally realizing that we were trapped, the High Command ordered us to blow up all our heavy equipment and make a quick retreat.

23

BETWEEN CHRISTMAS AND NEW YEAR OF 1944, our magnificent advance into the Grodno forest faded into a devastating retreat. The hardships of battle were made worse by freezing rain and heavy snow. When we could fight no longer, we faded into the Lipitchanian Forest, where our High Command ordered us to break into small groups and flee in different directions. That was our only hope to survive. We left our wounded behind, and many of them, not wanting to be captured alive, killed themselves.

It was a time of despair. The Germans had trapped us in a swampy area, and many of us drowned. Each of us tried to save himself; none of us helped his comrades. In fact, we fought each other off, saving our last bullets for self-preservation. Only we Jewish Partisans looked out for one another, terrified as we were of being captured by the Germans or the White Poles. In my group of about twenty-five men, we were constantly losing people to exposure and frostbite.

I was commanding a six-man squad. We had been assigned to a hill near a crossroads, where we manned a machine gun, covering our retreating forces. At one point I saw two tanks heading our way on one of the roads. I knew we wouldn't be able to stop a tank, so I sent a runner to notify our commanders of the situation, but he couldn't locate them. So we had to retreat.

We found our company commander, who demanded to know why I had ordered the retreat. He accused me of disobeying orders; he charged me with neglect, abandoning my post, and allowing another company to be attacked by tanks. I was sure I would be facing a court martial. I tried to explain that I had retreated only to protect my men. I wouldn't have been able to stop the tanks. To my huge relief, no charges were brought against me, and my outstanding record remained untarnished.

On New Year's night we tried to cross the Niemen. We were fired on by White Poles and by our own forces, who in the darkness couldn't tell us from the enemy. I crossed the river on horseback and opened fire with my machine gun to protect our men from the White Poles' bullets. I was soaked to the skin and covered with ice, my clothing frozen solid. I had to let the horse go. Still I kept walking, holding on to my machine gun, by then a worthless chunk of frozen metal.

Yet not long after those terrible days and nights, it became clear that the war was turning in our favor. Our bulletins were full of propaganda about Red Army victories. News began reaching us about the Allies' victories on the western front. The first months of 1944 brought back hope and our will to live. The only questions that remained were how long victory would take and who would survive until it came.

Fighting ferociously, the Germans shelled our *ziemlankas*. It was impossible for us to leave the forest. In all that chaos I was named commander of a platoon of Jewish fighters. I was happy to be promoted but leery of being segregated in this way. Needing more fighting men, I looked for recruits in the family camp. Some of the men who joined my platoon helped me search for provisions, which we needed badly. To reach the family camp we had to trek ten kilometers, following a dangerous path through swampland.

The family camp was somewhat more protected than the warriors' camp, being isolated by a swamp; even so, the people there were suffering horribly. Typhus had broken out among them, and no medical help at all was available. My men and I helped them out however we could.

Scouting for food, we stopped at a farm and coaxed the farmer into giving us whatever he could spare. He happily lent us a wagon, but not before loading it with a sack of potatoes, a sack of corn flour, four chickens, eggs, butter, cheese, two smoked hams, and two big loaves of freshly baked bread. On top of all this, he gave us some moonshine—an important requirement of life on the farms and in the forests. I promised to return the horse and wagon, not wanting to poison a good source of future supplies. With the help of Leib and Kalmanowitch, we hauled the supplies across the treacherous swamp to the family camp.

At the family camp I met a pretty, intriguing girl named Sonia. She was highly regarded by my friends, who shared a hut with her, her father, and her little brother. When I set eyes upon her, tenderness was rekindled in my heart. There was no time for romance in the middle of a swamp in the middle of a forest in the middle of a raging war. But I couldn't help hoping I would meet her again.

Few people survived the family camps, and if the Red Army hadn't advanced so quickly, no one at all would have. The same was true for the Underground fighters. Besides battling the Germans without cease, we suffered our own typhus epidemic, which claimed many lives. I caught it myself and suffered from its nosebleeds, high fever, and weight loss. When I was finally able to walk again, I had to support myself on crutches.

Once I was on my feet again, my biggest fear was of being unarmed. My weapons had been taken from me when I got sick. As soon as I could stand again I volunteered for a mission just to get my guns back. I could hardly walk, much less keep up with the brigade, but I was determined not to fall behind. After a night march I fell sick again, shivering with fever. The doctor gave me a shot of brewer's yeast, and that helped me regain my physical strength, but emotionally I was in shambles after I learned how many of my friends had been killed in these final battles.

The orders from Moscow were for the local brigades to hold their positions and attack the German army as it retreated through the Lipitchanian Forest. Contingents from Kapustin's brigades were leaving for the Grodno area every day. One day I was ordered to join them, and so I lost contact with Sonia.

Operation Rail War had been planned as a synchronized effort of all the Underground units. At a predetermined time, every Underground fighter was to help derail a train. Our brigade was assigned to the area between Mosty and Grodno. Each of us carried a square bar of TNT and a detonating capsule, which was to be ignited with a cigarette. Each TNT bar was to be attached to the rail by a magnet.

I was with my brigade when we heard a train approaching. We could tell from the sound that it was a locomotive with one car, following the line to check for mines or explosives. The train stopped, and soldiers left the car to examine the footprints leading away from the rails. While they were examining the footprints, we fired on them and cut them all down. The soldiers out of the way, we placed our explosives at the designated hour and retreated to safety.

While we were fading back we heard our mines explode and looked up to watch chunks of the rail line flying all over the place and fiery debris floating down through the dark. It was good to see; we Partisans were still a force to be reckoned with. Praise for our successful mission came from as far away as Moscow. A special bulletin praising the Underground was issued to us over the signature of Stalin himself. Soon the news reached us that the Red Army had liberated the areas around Slonim and Baranovich.

We were ordered to occupy various small settlements around Grodno while some of us advanced into the forests around Bialystok. With twenty men under my command, we started out early in the morning to place explosives between Lida and Grodno. Our job done, the TNT capsules attached to their targets, we returned to camp. Civilians we met along the way told us the Red Army was already in the neighborhood. I worried that if the Red Army soldiers began following the road we had just mined, they might become the victims of our work. So I quickly gathered my men and we hurried back to where we had planted the mines. There we saw two burning trucks and a number of injured Red Army soldiers. The mines we had planted only hours before had caused this mayhem.

I was horrified and didn't know what to do. I wanted to greet our liberators and lend them a hand. Though I feared the consequences, I decided to face these new arrivals. When the Russian soldiers saw us approaching they ordered us to drop our weapons.

"We are Soviet Partisans," I tried to explain. Stepping forward, I dropped to my knees and kissed their leader's hand, tears streaming down my face. "Sergeant," I told him, "it's my fault these men were injured. We were fighting the retreating Nazis and didn't know the Red Army was so close."

"We're fighting a war," the sergeant said with obvious lack of sympathy. He ordered us to help carry the injured to a farm settlement for first aid.

It took ten days to free Grodno. There were many German snipers around, shooting at anything that moved. We searched for them from house to house. In one house my Jewish friends and I found three Gestapo soldiers hiding in a pile of straw. It was a pleasure to tell these Nazis, who were pleading for their lives, that they had been captured by three Jews, and ghetto survivors at that. To our regret, we weren't permitted to kill them. Later, at the POW camp, when we were asked how our prisoners had been so badly beaten, we told our commander the Nazis hadn't appreciated being captured by Jews.

At last the Germans were defeated. A civil government was being established under the Red Army. The Soviet commissars formed a people's militia to help them draft young people between eighteen and forty-five years of age. The Poles in the district resented the Soviet mobilization, especially because the Underground, in cooperation with military intelligence units, had been tasked with rounding up draft dodgers.

My platoon marched a group of sixty draftees from Grodno to Mosty. There I delivered ten inductees to a colonel; the rest had deserted along the way. I spoke with the colonel, and to my surprise he greeted me warmly with the very common greeting among Jews: "Shalom Aleichem." He cried as he listened to the story of my survival and of my life as a Partisan. Meeting a Jewish high-ranking officer in the Red Army was overwhelming to me, a Partisan survivor.

Life was chaotic in those first days under the Soviets. I returned to Minsk and eventually found our battalion and my former commander. There was no order to life yet, but my fighting with the Partisans was recognized. I was awarded two medals for bravery as a Soviet Partisan and was promised I would be paid for my services as a noncommissioned Soviet officer. With the medals but no money in my pocket, I returned with Valodya to Baranovich. Having been promised jobs by an NKVD officer we had met, we presented ourselves in Baranovich. There was no housing to be found in the devastated city, so the officer put us up in his office building for the two days it took for us to register for work.

We also were provided with travel permits, and I went with Valodya to visit his family. The warm concern of Valodya's mother awakened me to my own reality: I was alone in the world, with no family or true friends. Where was I to turn? Where could I find a roof over my head, equality as a citizen, and a way to establish a decent life according to my own traditions, beliefs, and principles? During the war I had used force, weapons, and my warrior status to force other people to fill my immediate needs. Always suspicious, always distrustful, I had lived a rootless life. Now I had been discharged and stripped of my weapons, and I was left feeling insecure and defenseless. The war was over; it was time to begin acting like a human again.

After liberation I saw people gathering in prayer to thank the Almighty for ending the war. The devastated cities, the unburied corpses, the crippled and injured, the ashes of the bombed out villages—the living misery I encountered on the way to Minsk—did not awaken me to express gratitude to God for being alive. I was angry and could not bring myself to plan a new life based on the ideals of the past. I felt trapped. There was no one even to notify that I had survived. The lime-covered graves of Jews in the forest of Grodno jarred my memories awake and almost drove me mad. I had survived but I was beginning to doubt whether I wanted to continue along my parents' path and begin life once more as a Jew.

All at once I wanted no part of being remembered. I did not want to be reminded of how lucky I had been to survive as a Jew. I was haunted by the urge to hide my Jewish identity, to distance myself from Jewish ways, to get away to some unknown place where I would not be known as a Jew. I stopped looking for old friends and stopped looking for Jews to make new friends. I thought about staying with Valodya and restarting my life as a Gentile. I felt comfortable working on his farm and being treated like a human being. I went to parties with Valodya every night and joined in the drinking. Never there was I referred to as "the Jew."

Then one Sunday while Valodya and his family were getting ready for church, I suddenly understood that I did not belong there. Valodya noticed my discomfort and suggested I visit the Jews in Derechin. His remark sobered me and led me to change my plans. I remembered that I could not hide from myself among Gentiles. I would be kidding myself if I tried.

Valodya and I climbed onto the wagon and started out for Derechin. As we journeyed down the same roads I had traveled so long ago during my escape from the ghetto, the blood rushed to my head. My heart beat rapidly as we passed by the big pit I had been forced to help dig. The ghetto came alive in my mind; I saw shadows of ghosts and spirits greeting my arrival. We turned toward the Jewish cemetery. I wanted to visit the graves of my father and grandparents. But even the dead had not been left in peace: the cemetery had been desecrated, and there was no way to find the graves of my elders. My façade of courage collapsed, and I began to cry, for my parents, my grandparents, my whole family that had been so cruelly destroyed by the barbarian Nazis. And I cried for myself, alone, the wandering Jew.

I parted from Valodya, my friend. As he drove away, he looked back and waved for a long time. I knew I would not be returning this way and that we would never see each other again. Dejected, I stood at the fence surrounding the mass graves. A passerby came over to see who this man in a uniform was who had been standing still so long. It was Ivan, the man who had given us breakfast so very long ago when as Partisans we had reclaimed Derechin from the Nazi garrison.

Ivan invited me to his home and offered me food and drink. "You drink like a Russian and not like a Jew," his wife told me. The sarcasm in her voice convinced me even more that there was no love left for Jews among these people.

Pops, the elder Kviat, another Derechin Jew who had survived, came to see me at Ivan's when he heard I was there. He even remembered my nickname, "Shikorski." He told me that most of the surviving young men had been drafted before they had a chance to return to Derechin.

Three girls from our Underground brigade had also returned to Derechin, and I stayed with them until I left for Baranovich. They were glad to have me, for there were plenty of former collaborators in Derechin who were ready to eliminate those who had witnessed their collaboration. I knew full well that my family had been annihilated, yet I still checked with all the Gentiles who would have remembered them—had one or two perhaps escaped the slaughter? But asking the question only made me feel worse.

And it enraged me that the local Gentiles had taken over the property of the slaughtered Jews, and that they clearly weren't willing to return it. It was grotesque how angry they became when they encountered Jewish survivors. Besides not wanting to give up their loot, they feared being sent to Siberia as collaborators. Many were ready to kill any returning Jews.

This visit to Derechin was my homage to the souls of my ancestors. Just the same, I decided never to return to this place, where I had lost my family, my heritage, and my innocence.

The city of Baranovich had been largely destroyed. The skeletons of charred buildings stood mute guard over the carnage; the smell of burned flesh buried in the rubble assaulted my nose. It was a nightmare.

In all this chaos, with the Soviet military trying to run the city, I began looking for work, floating from office to office, Eventually I landed in the office of the commander of the employment division of the regional NKVD. There I learned quickly that Captain Trussov, head of the finance department, was also a Jew. Trussov greeted me with the familiar "Shalom Aleichem" and saw that I was issued food stamps. He also got me enrolled in a bookkeepers' training course and found me work as a bookkeeper for the NKVD quartermaster's office. Even the mighty Red Army couldn't find a bed for me, so for a time I used my office desk as a bed and living quarters.

Captain Trussov told me that young men like myself should feel obligated to go to school and train to become NKVD investigators. "The country needs men like you," he told me. It was tempting, but I thought better of it, explaining that I would rather pursue a career in bookkeeping, a profession I already knew something about. I wasn't much impressed with the equipment on his desk—an abacus and some antique business machines.

He took me to the transportation yard to explain my new job to me. I was going to be a dispatcher. There were twenty vehicles in the garage—a collection of Russian, German, and American trucks, passenger cars, and station wagons. There was a repair shop on the premises, where I would be approving the needed parts and repairs and monitoring gasoline and oil use. I would also be managing the payroll of the drivers and mechanics. Difficulties arose when drivers broke speedometers to cover up the fact that they were operating vehicles and consuming gasoline for personal reasons.

While working there, within the web of Soviet bureaucracy, I attended NKVD school. I also helped round up draftees and helped pursue former collaborators, who were hiding in the same forests that once hid the Partisans. In other words, I continued hunting down Black Crows even after the war, except this time it was they who were hiding in the forests, not us.

On my first day off from work I met a man named Shimon. He, too, was the only survivor from his family, having survived the war in a family camp in the Baranovich Forest. We struck up a conversation, and when he heard I had no real place to stay, he invited me to stay with him. A shared wooden platform covered with straw and a horsehair blanket were an improvement over my desk. Shimon and I became good friends. Together we went to the bathhouse to be deloused and have our underclothes washed. Through him I encountered other Jews from the Partisan brigades who were getting together for Sabbath dinners and to celebrate the High Holy Days.

Shimon, an optimist by nature, did his best to cheer me up. Every time the Red Army won a major victory, he infused me with hope that the war would soon be over and that we wouldn't be drafted. Through him I met an old friend, Sholom Shniadovich, who had been a neighbor of my family in my hometown of Ostrolenka. He invited me to join him and his wife at their Sabbath table.

Slowly I was beginning to understand that I could not peel away my Jewish roots, that I could not divest myself of all the traditions I had learned from my parents and grandparents, that my old values would have to be part of the new life I was beginning to build. I felt a desire to go back to my roots, and I realized there was no place for me, a Jew, in this part of Europe. The Soviets would never accept me as one of their own.

I was beginning to notice that in the Soviet Union all were not equal. Even without a rank, I was being permitted to eat in the officers' dining room, yet I would have been hungry still if Captain Trussov hadn't allotted me extra food coupons. Winter was approaching, and I had no warm clothes. Furthermore, Shimon had been drafted, so I had lost the roof over my head. I was forced to move in with a Soviet family. Though I put up with the lack of privacy and tried hard to get along with them, they deeply resented my presence and blamed me for all their troubles. It was time for me to find a way around the benefits of Soviet kindness and equality.

24

DURING THAT TROUBLED WINTER I again ran into Sonia Haidukowski. My heart pounded when I saw the pretty girl with the rosy cheeks and downcast eyes, who had awakened tender feelings in me when I first met her in the family camp in the Lipitchanian Forest. She was living in Zshetel with her father and brother, working as a typesetter for a local bulletin.

My life began to change with the New Year. I became determined to settle down and marry. I began corresponding with Sonia, expressing my admiration for her and for the understanding I found in her replies.

We both felt the need to be closer to each other physically and emotionally. Soon in our letters we began expressing a desire to marry and be together. But our present circumstances wouldn't allow it. I was working for the Russian authorities in Baranovich, and Sonia was miles away in Zshetel, so transportation was a nightmare.

To improve our chances of being together, I approached my boss for a transfer to Zshetel. He turned me down flat, pointing out that there was a war on and that he had no one to replace me. Sonia then asked for a transfer to Baranovich, and this request, too, was refused. Swallowing our annoyance, we continued our romance through the mail. Marriage would have to wait.

Around that time, the Soviet authorities notified all Polish-born individuals who had lived in Poland before the war that they would be permitted to return to Poland. These individuals were to register with the authorities. Not many of them did; the Soviets had been known to mislead, misinform, and misguide. Also, some people, like myself, were working for the Soviets and so not free to leave. Some of my Jewish friends advised me to register under an assumed name and flee illegally when the time came. I was engaged to Sonia and did not want to leave without her, so I asked her if she would return to Poland with me. Of course she was all for it, *after* we were married.

Not wanting to be seen in person, I had someone go in my place to the Commission for the Return of Polish Citizens to register in my name to receive a Polish passport.

Since I couldn't travel to Zshetel to discuss marriage with her, I asked Sonia's father to come to Baranovich, where we could talk face to face. Graciously he came, and he consented to the marriage. He knew his daughter loved me, he said, and he would not stand in our way.

We set a date for the wedding: January 5, 1945. Without permission from my superiors, I traveled to Zshetel on January 4. We were married the next day in a religious ceremony. The civil marriage license would come later.

The day after our marriage, I heard that the NKVD had a warrant to arrest me. I would be better off, my source told me, if I turned myself in at Baranovich instead of being arrested in Zshetel. So I returned to Baranovich. So much for our honeymoon, which had lasted three days.

When I reported back at my office in Baranovich I was ordered to surrender my weapons and placed under arrest for desertion. My good standing with the colonel, head of the regional NKVD, who intervened on my behalf, saved me from jail. Standing up for me, he blamed the captain, my boss, for not permitting me time for marriage.

In fact, I came out of the escapade quite well. I was assigned to travel to Minsk once a month, for three or four days each time. While in Minsk I could sneak away to Zshetel and spend some time with my wife.

May 10, 1945, my twenty-third birthday, coincided with VE Day. I would remember that day as the greatest of my life. Army bands were playing; speeches were made glorifying the Soviet leaders; parades were held even bigger than the ones on Revolution Day.

But my joy was marred when my boss confronted me. "Gregory Ickevitz, you wear medals bestowed on you by the Red Army; you work for the NKVD. Did you think you could get away with registering to return to Poland?"

Trying to outsmart him, I retorted, "Comrade Captain, it was officially announced that the Poles are our allies. Besides, I never registered. Maybe it was my wife who did."

He replied that he could pin down not only the day I registered but also the time, and he demanded that I withdraw the registration. As brave as I tried to act, I was terrified of being arrested again and facing some trumped up charges.

I sent Sonia a message to be ready to escape. On my next official trip to Minsk, we finalized our plans. We returned to Baranovich on May 12, 1945, and quietly boarded a train for Bialystok, where we hid with friends for a time. Taking their advice, we continued to Lodz, a large city in Poland to which many survivors of the concentration camps were returning. In Lodz, with the help of a man I knew from Baranovich, I tried my hand at some black marketeering, just to keep us going. In Lodz we heard about a Zionist group that was smuggling people out of Europe. We approached these emissaries for help in escaping this accursed continent, the cemetery of all our families.

I had belonged to a Zionist organization before the war. I contacted the Hashomer Hatzair group, and we gave ourselves over to their instructions. In groups of four we would travel to Krakow; two days later we would continue to Prague. In Prague we would board trains for Budapest however we could. There, representatives from the American Joint Distribution Committee would smuggle us into Austria, and on from there.

While in Poland I had a narrow escape; I was spotted by a Russian NKVD major who had known me in Baranovich. It was the last straw; over Sonia's wishes, I made my mind up that we would leave Poland without waiting for her family.

The lodging and food along our route was provided to us by American volunteers. The ex-Partisans, being men of the gun, were not happy sitting idle. There was an incident in Hungary when ten of our people burst into the AJDC offices demanding immediate action. The demonstration worked, and we were able to leave Hungary. We crossed the Mur River near Klagenfurt, Austria. As our group's appointed leader, I was detained by the Soviets; fortunately, they released me after two days. We continued to Graz, which was in the British zone, and registered in a Displaced Persons camp.

It was heartbreaking to encounter our new comrades, emaciated survivors of the concentration camps who once again had found themselves living in camps. We were all waiting for the AJDC and the Zionist organizations to help us leave this camp for the ancient and promised land of Israel.

During our stay in the DP camp, we met soldiers serving in the Jewish Brigade of the British Army. It warmed our hearts to meet these proud, heroic Jews, who visited us to encourage us in our struggles. They stirred up dormant emotions, unmet hopes of reaching the Promised Land. They told us about missions they had fought in against the Nazis. The Star of David insignia shining on their trucks and uniforms inspired us to hope for a brighter future. The humiliating Star of

David we had been forced to wear by the barbarian Nazis had been re-placed by the hope and pride we felt at the sight of these Jewish soldiers serving the mighty British Army. With the help of the Jewish Brigade, some of us were transported to refugee camps in Italy.

I found myself caught in a whirlwind of idealism, consumed by a desire to help actively in the immigration effort. That is how I became an organizer in the refugee camps, over the objections of Sonia, who was by then expecting a baby.

Through my work with Aliya Beth, I had been promised legal pas-sage to Israel, and I was disappointed when that promise fell through. So I made up my mind to emigrate to the United States.

Our daughter, Rosalie, arrived on April 6, 1946, in Florence, Italy, where we were waiting for our U.S. immigration papers. Many DPs were arriving in Italy at the time and being housed at a camp near Modena. Alongside that camp was another that held former Nazis; their proxim-ity inflamed us, the Jewish survivors, and led to brawls with the POWs. Eventually we were moved to another location, away from the Nazis.

When Hashomer Hatzair gained control of the refugees' leader-ship, I was one of the representatives on the ballot. We managed to sep-arate the orphans from the families, place them under the supervision of philanthropic organizations, and have them transferred to a separate camp. Special care was given to sick people and pregnant women. For teenagers, vocational schools were established, and for adults, retrain-ing programs in different trades. After two weeks of tenacious effort, with outside help, we had completely reorganized the camp at Modena.

The leaders of the Rome camp, having heard about our success, vis-ited us to learn our methods. Soon many camps were asking us to send volunteers to help them reorganize. We arranged seminars for those who wished to remain in the camp and prepare our people for Israel. Though our goals were the same, rivalries began creeping into the ideo-logical factions. The men who had fought in the Underground were now an aggressive political force. They believed in using force to reclaim our land, whereas others preached different methods to attain the goal.

I volunteered to participate in a seminar and was sent to Milan. For four weeks I attended lectures, listened to speeches of Histadrut leaders, and was indoctrinated into the ideology of my party, Hashomer Hatzair. When I finished, they assigned me to be the leader of a *kibbutz* that was training people as farmers. It was gratifying to see the people who had depended on the DP camp to survive become productive beings enthusiastically preparing for a future in Israel.

Sonia and I were disappointed that we would not be able to join the groups being smuggled into Palestine. Pregnant women and families with children were not permitted to make the risky sailing, with the British intercepting illegal ships. We were more than willing to wait, safe with our baby.

Throughout the war years the U.S. address of my Aunt Esther, my mother's sister, had stayed in my memory. Now I was a family man, a father. Unable to emigrate to Israel as I had planned, I contacted my Aunt Esther for help. Even though my organization still needed me as a *kibbutz* leader, I returned to Florence to await a reply from my American relatives.

Villa Almansi and Silvia were two DP camps near Florence supervised by UNRA. Both were for families with babies. There was a woman, Madame Casino, who was very helpful to the young refugee mothers in the DP camps. There we sat waiting to hear from our families. Mail was still very sporadic, the best source being the American and British armies stationed in Italy. A letter came from Aunt Esther full of love and gladness that I had survived. She remembered me as a child and was anxious for us to be reunited.

The monotonous waiting in Italy finally ended when President Truman's new bill lifted many restrictions and increased the immigration quota for DPs.

In every camp and in every city and every corner of the world, the morale of Jews reached a peak with the creation of a Jewish homeland, the State of Israel. There were also tears of sorrow; so many had given their young lives to achieve rebirth, independence, and freedom for the handful who had survived the war.

In January 1948 our visas arrived. The *Vulcania* brought us to the blessed shores of the United States on March 14, 1948. Our hearts beat faster as we passed the Statue of Liberty with its torch, the symbol of liberty and justice, raised high. We entered the harbor of safety, eagerly anticipating a life of freedom.

My reunion with my relatives in Chicago, and especially my Aunt Esther, was extremely emotional. I watched her eyes as I introduced her to my wife and handed her our little baby. I held back my tears; I didn't know how to tell her about our losses, our suffering, the bestial treatment of our people at the hands of the Nazi beasts. She knew about the six million Jewish men, women, and children lost. She looked at our baby without speaking, tears streaming down her face. She was able to comfort the child in me, the child she had known way back in Ostrow-Mazowiecka. Her warmth, her charm, and her love were a balm to my soul, soothing the past that even now invades my dreams. Throughout the years we were in close contact, she loved me like my own mother.

Epilogue

I HAVE TRIED TO KEEP MY PROMISE to relate the disaster that befell my family and my people, a memory that will stay with me forever.

My family and I consider ourselves lucky to have reached the blessed shores of freedom and democracy in the United States of America. My life in my adopted country has not been without struggles and hardships; nevertheless, it has been satisfying. It has been a life without danger, a life of freedom. We have been able to live in dignity as Jews.

Sonia and I became parents again, to a wonderful son, Michael. He and Rosalie helped us establish roots in this land. Rosalie and her husband, Jeffery, have presented us with three wonderful grandchildren, Jennifer, Marisa, and Jordan. Michael and Susan have added to our family two wonderful grandsons, Scott and Mark.

The greatest pleasures we know are our three great-grandchildren, Emily, Matthew, and Daniel, our granddaughter Jennifer's children, and Marisa and Ben's son Noah.

We are grateful to God for our blessings, and we bless our country, the precious United States of America.